Norms and Human Behavior

Arnold Birenbaum
**Albert Einstein College of Medicine of
Yeshiva University**

Edward Sagarin
**The City College of
the City University of New York**

PRAEGER PUBLISHERS
New York

Published in the United States of America in 1976
by Praeger Publishers, Inc.
111 Fourth Avenue, New York, N.Y. 10003

Library of Congress Cataloging in Publication Data
Birenbaum, Arnold.
  Norms and human behavior.

  Bibliography: p. 166
  Includes index.
  1. Deviant behavior. 2. Social control. I. Sag-
arin, Edward, 1913–   joint author. II. Title.
HM291.B478   301.6'2   74–2688
ISBN 0–275–52090–0
ISBN 0–275–85060–9 pbk.

Printed in the United States of America

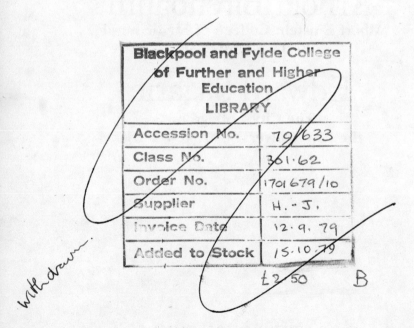

To my father, Max Birenbaum
—Arnold

To my son, Fred L. Sagarin
—Edward

Contents

Preface

This book is a result of the authors' many years of teaching, discussion, and research on the subject of conformity and deviance. Both of us had discovered that undergraduate students are as interested in issues of conformity and its constraints as they are fascinated by rule-violating behavior. We have attempted to raise and answer some questions about these basic aspects of organized social life. It is our hope that by providing a unified approach to this subject we will encourage students to think about conformity and deviance as outcomes of social interaction.

Both of us have written about conformity as well as deviance, and we found it useful to incorporate revised versions of some of our previously published material in this book. A study on social interaction among prospective jurors, by Birenbaum, originally published in *Criminology: An Interdisciplinary Journal,* is incorporated here. Some of the sections on deviance are adapted from a recent textbook on that subject by the second author. This book is a new contribution to introductory sociology and to the study of social behavior, concerning the questions: Why do people create rules? Why do some follow rules? Why do some violate the rules?

We wish to thank Arthur Vidich, of the New School for Social Research, and Jerry Rose, of the State University of New York at Fredonia, for their thoughtful criticism and suggestions during the preparation of the manuscript. As in the past, we admire and appreciate the work of Gladys Topkis, our superb editor.

A.B.
E.S.

Norms and Human Behavior

1

Norms and Social Life

Sociology is a discipline that studies the basic aspects of how people live in groups, how they deal with one another or relate to one another. The sociologist tries to assess whether these relationships provide freedom for individuals to grow and be secure or limit choice and individual development. The consequences of these social relationships are not inevitable or unalterable; yet they are patterned and often predictable. Social life is highly organized because human beings are social beings who not only react to sensations but also interpret what others say and do. This patterning is made possible by the existence of certain rules and regulations that govern human behavior.

The word "norm" is generally used by sociologists to describe the guides for human conduct that are accepted in a given situation at a given time. A more detailed and precise definition of the term will be presented later in this chapter; it is introduced here because it will be used frequently in a discussion of the place of compliance and violation in making society possible. Suspending for the moment the effort to examine the definitions of sociolo-

1

gists, let us think of norms as socially expected and accepted forms of conduct.

According to the great German sociologist Max Weber, human action is social in character insofar as it takes into account the existence of other people, their expected responses to one's behavior, and the shared meanings they place upon these actions. Blinking one's eye may be a reflex motion that takes place whether others are present or not. The identical physiological motion may be done in a specific social situation, with certain other actors, in response to social stimuli; in this case it is a social act called winking and has a very special meaning. Social acts are patterned because meaning is bestowed upon them by two or more people and sometimes through the development of permanent ways of doing things. When patterns of behavior in a society are directed toward the satisfaction of basic human needs, we speak of the behavior as institutionalized and of the cluster of such fixed and expected conduct as a social institution. Existing institutions, such as the family or the economy, usually fulfill specific needs, but they may at the same time interfere with the fulfillment of other needs. However, the organized ways of doing things are not the only possible means of satisfying human needs, as is clearly indicated by the rich variety of ways in which people in diverse human societies assign work, develop faith and loyalty to the group, eat, sleep, mate, satisfy sexual drives, and defend themselves against real or imagined external enemies. At the very least, however, institutions do constitute organization and a way for human beings to orient themselves to one another.

As a result of the existence of social institutions, there is an excellent possibility that a person who occupies a position in a patterned relationship with others will have acquired some model of how other people will respond to him and, in turn, how he will respond to others. In short, the members of a society will have a similar set of expectations. These expectations may be merely implicitly understood by two people in a reciprocal relationship, so that they act in accordance with them without thinking about what they are doing. Sometimes the expectations become formal and explicit, as in a contract between a buyer and a seller. The expectations serve only as guidelines or boundaries to interaction, because humans are capable of reacting in a variety of ways to what others are doing or saying, and each response causes alterations in the words and deeds of others. The new responses of others must then cause alterations in one's own set or repertory of rejoinders. Through this process, people arrive at shared definitions of situations, anticipating what would happen if they did not do something and predicting what others expect them to do. Human beings can simultaneously act and observe their action. To observe his own behavior, a person must place himself mentally or metaphorically in the position of the other—a competency that George Herbert Mead (1934 ed.) called "taking the role of the other."

By virtue of this human quality of treating oneself as an object of observation, people can also learn new expectations, which they were not involved in creating. Thus expectations can be transferred to newcomers through role taking. What were implicitly understood expectations can become independent from the person who originally created them and crystallize into rules or norms, which all persons in certain social categories are expected to follow. Institutionalization can be further defined—without in any sense conflicting with our previous definition—as a set of social expectations that clearly state which activities are to be performed and by whom, the rewards for fulfilling these expectations, and the costs of not fulfilling them. Moreover, persons who occupy these positions must also be provided with some explanation as to why these activities must be performed in the specified way and only by certain people. These justifications or rationales bestow a special quality upon very common human practices, giving them an almost sacred character, so that people get upset or outraged when things are done differently. It is this sacred character that gives institutions the appearance of being permanent and unalterable although they are only human constructions, often fragile, always malleable.

Finally, institutions acquire permanency over extended periods of time when there is a method devised to transmit the specifics of who does what and why to newcomers not involved in the original formation of the institution. As the people who occupy positions in the institution transmit the expectations to those unfamiliar with them, the expectations become rules or norms to be respected and complied with, not merely to be followed as guidelines. Because these rules have lost contact with their originators, they have a kind of immutable quality about them.

While one may have to learn specific rules in order to perform within a particular institutional area, most people are aware that rules exist in all areas of life and take them into account when engaged in or anticipating interaction with other people. This awareness is part of the organized character of social life. Rules, then, do not have to be inculcated in people in order to be obeyed. The human capacity to take the role of the other makes it possible to bridge the gaps among those who do not have common experiences. Moreover, even when people dislike or reject a rule, it may be extremely difficult for them not to obey it, for much of everyday life involves opportunities to demonstrate social competency, a factor that may override the will to disobey. Often obedience to the rule is simply reflexive, whereas transgression is effortful. Consider how difficult it is not to say hello to a person you do not like when he passes you on the street, or not to say "Excuse me," after sneezing in public, as discussed later under the concept of the sanctions for noncompliance.

The organization of our everyday world is tied to the people we know, even those we hate. People with whom territory is shared, even for brief periods of time, provided that they have a right to be there, are classified as familiar, even when they are enemies. In turn, strangers who are not expected to be present in certain places or on certain occasions are defined as unfriendly or threatening until they account for their presence and give evidence that they are harmless.

We have noted that one does not have to agree with a rule to obey it. Nor does one have to disagree with a rule to be regarded as a "deviant," a term that will be defined presently. A person may conform to avoid immediate punishment or to maintain his his right to group membership. In contrast, a physically disabled person may be excluded from a group even when he wants to belong. It all depends on the particular situation; rules or norms are based on the expectations that are held for the participants.

Sometimes one speaks of the participants as being "members," not only in the narrow sense of belonging to a group or society, but also in the sense of being one of the persons who are supposed to be present. Social situations provide clues to the expectations for participants. In modern society there is a great deal of contact among people who do not know each other, and this makes it all the more essential that rules be spelled out, along with the punishments that will be visited upon violators and the rewards granted to those who conform.

Norms are both proscriptive and prescriptive. The former are those that forbid an action; they can be traced back to the Ten Commandments, in which people are admonished in the words: "Thou shalt not . . ." Proscriptive norms are often accompanied by a warning that tells the potential violator just what the penalties will be if he does not obey. Signs in a zoo may read: "Keep off the grass—$25 fine." Prescriptive norms, on the other hand, can be described as more positive in the sense that they tell us what we should do, such as provide the necessities for our children, including the affection they require. Prescriptive norms, when followed, often bring approval from others or even from oneself, a self-recognition that one is being virtuous or at least doing the right thing. Sometimes proper behavior is rewarded through contests in which civil servants, such as bus drivers, are given prizes for being courteous.

Even if all people were perfect because of some innate goodness or successful training, there would still be a societal need to recognize conformity and deviance. These acts of recognition, according to the great French sociologist Emile Durkheim (1933 ed.), reaffirm the dependency of human beings on one another as members of society. For Durkheim, norms provided the proper subject matter of sociology because they were "external and constraining" to people, representing society to the individual. In themselves, norms are idealizations, activated only when they are enforced. If it is true, as seems apparent, that without norms there would be no society, it is also true, although not always so obvious, that without rule-breaking society would likewise be close to impossible. For failure to conform produces the recognition among the conforming members of society of their dependence on generally accepted and respected rules and regulations.

The activation of a norm or set of norms always takes place within a social context in which members of a special group define rule-breaking or the rule-breaker as a danger to the group and themselves. Some practices in the business world, such as bribery, may not be regarded as deviant because they have become accepted ways of behaving in the business context. At the same time, it can hardly be said that business people prefer bribery to honesty. Some entrepreneurs feel they have no choice but to use money to help make more money. Bribery may be tolerated without being desired or preferred. The practice is based on the common perception that competitors can and will take advantage of someone who tries to live up to an ideal of pure goodness.

Informal norms created in face-to-face interaction often displace the formally conceived and idealized rules found in organizations. When soldiers live together in combat situations, parade-ground discipline is not practiced. The relaxation of rigid rules, whether in corporation, hospital, armed services, or even prison, takes place essentially for three reasons.

First, informal group standards are relatively easy to enforce because other members of the group provide an immediate reaction to those who break the rules. In contrast, formal norms often involve rather remote rewards and punishments. Failure to comply with an informal norm can also involve loss of self-esteem and acceptance as a member among peers. Persons in work groups, for example, may set up rules for production independent of what the management conceives to be production goals. Worker-created rules establishing "a fair day's work for a fair day's pay" are enforced in face-to-face interaction by ridicule or sarcasm directed at those who overproduce. Sometimes those who do not comply are subject to more coercive efforts to enforce the rules, which prevent them from working at a slower or faster pace.

Second, compliance with informal norms provides social support for individuals who have little idea of where they stand in an organization in which supervision and evaluation may be rather abstract and remote. Group membership and compliance offer security and immediate feedback on the question of how well one is doing and whether he is measuring up to the ideal, or at least to an acceptable version of the ideal. Often formal organizations develop new rules that promote direct supervision and evaluation. While this may seem to be a great improvement in the efficiency of the organization, it can also interfere with the accomplishment of its goals by encouraging the development of techniques to conceal behavior from all those responsible for evaluation. The workers may adopt these techniques in an attempt to continue to be as effective as they were before despite the new rule rather than because they want to see the organization fail.

Third, new formal rules, imposed from above or by persons considered to be outsiders, are often added to old practices. Old hands who were not consulted or who are familiar with a different set of practices that fulfills their needs may resent this intrusion. Consequently, they might not feel obliged to obey rules established by people they see as not having a right to guide their behavior.

The extent to which compliance is regarded as obligatory varies from situation to situation and rule to rule. During times of scarcity the Eskimo elderly may end their lives on an ice floe, but they are less constrained to do so when food is plentiful. Rules concerned with the preservation of the group and its members are generally regarded as having a higher degree of obligation associated with them than rules that relate merely to technical practices. Being a traitor or a spy is much more serious than being a litterbug or a jaywalker, and no doubt is more serious than being an embezzler (except perhaps in the eyes of the victim). Loyalty is a characteristic expected to hold in all situations, even when one is tempted by dazzling opportunities. Going over to the other side, even under coercion, is considered to be an unspeakable act. The man who is without a country is not so despised as one who "sells out" his homeland to the enemy. Even the enemy who has recruited and profited from such a person is repelled by him. In a society where identities are rapidly shifting and large numbers of former outsiders are being assimilated into the mainstream, fear that the outsider may undermine national security through deception can become a major fixation.

Deviance, then, is separate from but nevertheless a part of group living. It produces occasions for reaffirmation of the norms in the entire rule-abiding group and for changing the norms when they no longer usefully serve the function for which they were created. Not all deviance provokes intervention by others; sometimes it is self-correcting. Rules and the violation of rules are bound together, and the two are intertwined with the life of a society and the lives of its members. But they are always part of the dynamics of a society, the ongoing struggle of the members to survive, the continuity and changes of dominant cultural patterns.

Minor Transgressions and Transgressors

Violations of norms occur frequently in everyday life, and competent people who commit some minor transgressions are able to correct themselves, often by separating themselves from the acts that violate the rules. Offering an apology is a simple way of acknowledging that a violation has occurred and expressing the violator's hope that others will continue to extend to him the same expectations for appropriate behavior in the future that they did in the past. Often a violation of the rules goes uncorrected because it does not come to the attention of someone else or because it is of no concern to the person who does observe it. In a modern society, with its many highly specialized institutions, it is not unusual for a given set of behaviors to be required in one context and prohibited in another. Thus a person may present two entirely different aspects of himself to two different audiences. This may be only a matter of demeanor—for example, of behaving in an authoritarian manner in an office where one has power but in a meek manner at home or at a social gathering. Or it can involve rules that are status-bound. For example, a physician is permitted to ask very personal questions of a patient and can touch the patient's body without hesitation and without asking permission, but such behavior toward the same individual would be intolerable under social rather than professional conditions.

The various aspects of a single individual's life may not be in harmony with one another, but even if this is apparent to others it may not lead them to condemn the individual. In the instance of the physician there is no conflict, for the world in which he moves has given recognition to his two statuses, as doctor and as family man and social mingler. But the father who neglects family duties for the sake of advancement on the company team is not the beneficiary of the same social approval. His activities may lead to criticism if not disapproval. Condemnation is not inevitable, however, for norms have their flexibility, they are tied to individuals as well as to statuses (so that some people can get away with more than others), all adding up to the fact that reactions to the violations are flexible, too.

Discrepancies between one's words and deeds may also go undiscovered if the social worlds in which a person circulates are kept apart and he is able to prevent them from coming into contact. Thus a man may boast to other men that he does nothing around the house, but he may actually be very much involved in sharing the housekeeping chores with his wife. People are often subjected to conflicting demands from others in different institutional and group contexts. They may manage these conflicting expectations quite well as long as the social situations in which they interact with others do not overlap. It can readily be understood that this situational variability permits one to present different sides of one's self to different people at different times.

One can also violate expectations repeatedly without coming to be regarded as someone who fails to meet the demands of others, when he can invoke generally recognized priorities to persuade others to reduce their demands. For example, to return to physicians, they are often called away from dinner parties to attend patients in an emergency, but certified public accountants cannot leave social occasions with that excuse. All those present at the dinner will agree that certain obligations take priority over others. Sometimes, when priorities are so evident, performers of certain roles can play off one partner against others, as when a teacher claims to students that administrative decisions prevent him from meeting their demands. In turn, teachers can tell administrators that enrollments will be reduced unless courses are made more appealing. Since administrative evaluation usually determines the teacher's future employment and promotion, most teachers will side with the more powerful interest. Again, the possible course of action is structured in advance by the person's prediction of the risks to himself and his partners.

In a very diverse society, it is possible that a great deal of deviance will be ignored in order to reduce social conflict among people. Modern societies are characterized by a highly refined division of labor and interdependency of different sectors of the society. If every violation of the society's norms were a matter of great concern, this would reduce the cooperation necessary to make that kind of specialization work effectively. Yet this very division of labor gives some subordinates the opportunity to curry favor in an organization by committing deviant acts without the explicit knowledge, but nevertheless with the approval, of their superiors. And then, with varying degrees of veracity and credibility, the superiors have a copout at their disposal: they can claim that there was no prior approval or even knowledge of what the subordinates had accomplished. Watergate and My Lai are notorious examples of what occurs, on a smaller and less significant scale, in the corporate, academic, military, and political worlds on countless occasions.

Before examining the motivations, patterns, and consequences of rule violation in society, let us look at the types of norms found in any social group and the manner in which people learn what the norms are and how they can become good social actors by following them.

DEFINITIONS, TYPOLOGIES, SOURCES

There are many definitions of norms. Sociologists have referred to them as "societal expectations," specifications of "appropriate and inappropriate behavior," "blueprints for behavior," and "rules of conduct." Jack Gibbs (1965), who has quoted, compared, and summarized these definitions, notes that the term *norm*, when used in a generic sense—that is, to cover all types of norms and all circumstances—must have three attributes. It must be

(1) a collective evaluation of behavior in terms of what it *ought* to be; (2) a collective expectation as to what behavior *will be;* and/or (3) particular *reactions* to behavior, including attempts to apply sanctions or otherwise induce a particular kind of conduct.

While no single definition of norms is "correct," we find it most useful to combine the first and second of these attributes, and then to assume that the behavior, if approved and accepted, is invariably supported by some sanction, no matter how slight, against transgressors. Thus norms may be thought of as legitimate socially shared guidelines to the accepted and expected patterns of conduct. Expectation alone would not make action normative; note, for example, the large number of people who commit automobile thefts and the social expectations of this behavior in the form of insurance, detectives, legal experts, engineers, and others who devote their time to the problem. The stealing of cars has come to be expected, and many people earn their living from this activity; yet car theft is not regarded by thieves or others as a preferred pattern of behavior. In the language of sociology, it can be said to lack legitimacy. While recruitment for this illegal occupation does occur, it is not done openly. Certainly it is not a guideline for social behavior, although it might be considered expected by various groups of people in society.

What if the behavior is accepted but not expected? Is it then normative? If it involves actions so infrequent that they are surprising, although welcome, one could hardly speak of the existence of a norm. Extremely polite action among strangers on subways in the large cities of the United States, for example, or giving all one's worldly goods to the poor are accepted but not expected. They are not deviant acts, but the infrequency of their occurrence results in a lack of patterned expectations.

Furthermore, infrequent social occasions may involve invoking a special set of legitimate rules to guide behavior. Ceremony is an important way to help people get through infrequent and unfamiliar social occasions because little latitude is left to the participants. Audiences with the Pope may require careful screening of participants and even rehearsals. Funerals and weddings provide examples of how ceremony helps people through these special social occasions. Clergy, ushers, pallbearers, and funeral directors try not to permit the major participants to make mistakes. While ceremony provides minute guides for behavior, other norms are generally far more flexible.

William Graham Sumner (1906), one of the major sociologists in the United States during the first decades of this century, divided norms into mores, laws, and folkways. Mores are those norms that express the strongest moral demands made on individuals in a society; folkways are the very pervasive and usually everyday actions that are widely accepted by the general populace. Later sociologists saw that these three categories, on the one hand, were insufficient to cover all norms and, on the other, were sometimes too broad in scope, needing further breakdown into—to mention a few other types—customs, shared morals, traditions, etiquette, ceremony, and ritual. True, some of these can become laws, others may involve mores, and etiquette, for example, can often be subsumed under folkways. In fact, mores and even folkways are at times codified into law. The categories thus are overlapping, yet are valuable in suggesting what various norms have in common, as well as how they differ.

The most generalized synonym for norm is rule. Both are guidelines for behavior. There is an important distinction, however, between rules and laws, both being norms. Laws are usually thought of as formal, explicit, politically enacted, and sanctioned by the legitimate use of force; in modern societies, they are also written. An organization, an employer, and even an informal friendship group may have rules of conduct that are backed by sanctions against the violator, but the fact that they are not enacted by a politically recognized body and are not supported by the force of a governmental authority gives them a different nature and different consequences. It is not merely the question of the ultimate use of force—a criminal group can murder a member for violation of a rule—but law involves legitimacy of enactment, a mechanism for the adjudication of the guilt or innocence of one accused of a violation, and, above all, the ultimate use of force and coercion by an armed body that acts as the enforcer and is the embodiment of the power of the state.

Norms have also been described as enacted or as crescive. The enacted norm is often synonymous with written law, or at least a specifically stated rule. "Crescive" means that the rule of behavior came about gradually, gaining solid popular support in stages, until an old rule had become obsolete and the new one had replaced it. Sociologists are concerned with crescive norms, for their existence raises some interesting and important questions in the analysis of social life. Did the first challenge to the old way incite anger and indignation? Was there a division within the society, along sex, age, race, or other lines, between the followers of the old and those of the new? Was there a technological change or development that preceded and precipitated a change in the norms?

Similar questions are raised with regard to enacted norms. Why did the enactment occur at a given time? Were there interest groups that crusaded for the enactment? Did the new norm meet resistance, or had the old ways lost their social base?

Finally, there is the knotty question of the relationship among laws, mores, and modes of behavior. What if the laws are in conflict with the mores? Is such a situation possible? We shall return to this question in a later chapter.

There are two aspects to the problem of the sources of norms. The first involves how particular norms originated; what were their sources in the history of a group or a society, why did a given way begin to take root, and how did it become part of the accepted ways of doing things, part of the shared patterns that some have summarized by the word "culture" and that Durkheim (1933 ed.) called the "collective conscience" of the people? The second involves the question of how these norms come to be communicated to individuals, how people come to know about them, accept them, and incorporate them into their own behavior patterns, and with what consequences this is accomplished.

Many of the rules of conduct are transmitted by custom and tradition, and as long as they work in a society, as long as technology and other developments do not make them obsolete, they retain their hold on the populace. Many of these are small, taken-for-granted parts of the daily routine: folkways or etiquette. In France, for example, a child gets up in the morning and shakes hands with his mother, father, sisters, and brothers; if we heard of this happening in an American home, we would think the people in that family were demented.

Norms are often borrowed from other societies. One can say that in recent decades, particularly as a result of a technology that brings people in greater contact with those whose ways are different, norms are not confined to the area where they first took hold. However, the question still remains: Why were people receptive to the new norms? Normative change may reflect other social changes. Max Weber stressed that norms change in the wake of great philosophical and ideological developments. In his classic work, *The Protestant Ethic and the Spirit of Capitalism* (1959 ed.), he found that the Protestant Reformation, particularly Calvinism, contained the roots of a new ethic, and that this brought new economic norms, especially in America: norms of thrift, persever- ance, love of toil, and others. Karl Marx, on the contrary, stressed the role of power, property distribution, ownership of the means of production, and class conflict in generating the normative behavior in a given society and the way in which societies are changed.

Despite all these rules, people often fail to meet expectations that others hold for them. Alternatively, people are constantly making new rules to prevent, control, or eliminate deviant behav- ior. Rule-making and rule-breaking behavior are part of group living, but the rules in themselves do not account for society. There is no one-to-one correspondence between the way things are and the way they are supposed to be. How, then, does orga- nized social life hold together?

How Is Society Possible?

Human beings, Charles Darwin tells us, are part of the order of nature. Yet human society is different from all other aspects of nature, including animal society, in part because of human awareness of consciousness, which contributes to the process that makes for order in society. People make and unmake the rules that help to make society possible. They are generally capa- ble of understanding how rules or social norms operate because in all their activities they are dependent on those with whom they share membership in a society. Starting at an early age, human beings develop strong social bonds with others and act in ways that take these bonds into account.

As we set it forth at the beginning of this chapter, people are observers of one another's actions as well as actors themselves. More important, they are observers of their own actions, and they pay a great deal of attention to how others seem to be perceiving these actions. This quality, which may be called reflexiveness, is an important aspect of human interaction.

This quality of mind, this social nature of human awareness, provides some partial answers to the question of what makes society possible and how social norms arise. Norms are social standards that depend on human activity to come into being. Unlike natural laws, norms do not operate independently of human participation. Rather, they are social constructions or conventions based on shared expectations. Rules come out of the day-to-day transactions in which people engage, and they guide the collective action of those who take part in these transactions. Consequently, rules are tied to a general sense of being part of something—a group, a gathering, a community, a society. All these collectivities, as sociologists call them, involve an awareness of who is to belong to them, who is to be excluded, and particularly what activities and deportment are to be expected of members.

The study of membership and nonmembership is one of the central features of sociology, but the significance of belonging lies in the way it is translated into behavior. Understanding membership and group identification therefore means understanding rules of conduct.

The concept of membership became important at the end of the eighteenth century, a time of extreme social and political instability. In that period, it was possible for some persons to break with at least some of the identities established by birth and to become—within limits, but to a much greater degree than heretofore—anything they wanted to be. If this was the case, how was it possible to hold a group together? Reflections on social stability became especially relevant during the industrial and French revolutions. Ironically, the study of conformity and deviance came to concern those who studied humanity just when individuals were transcending their traditional places in society.

Major thinkers of the late eighteenth and early nineteenth centuries, such as Edmund Burke and August Comte, remind us of how rules are used, not only to preserve group life, but also to preserve the individual as well, particularly in the face of rapid social changes. Being part of a collectivity meant then, as it means now, to be a member: norms articulate the nature of membership and nonmembership. Norms, then, have as much to do with a person's allegiances as with the coordination of conflicting interests, the prevention of traffic accidents, and the protection of the weak against the strong. Norms are not merely restrictions on human license but ways of displaying people's commitments, validating their social competency, and affirming their alignments to others.

As we have noted earlier, William Graham Sumner made distinctions among norms based on the degree to which the members of society regard the rules as highly valued and sacred. Norms were characterized in Sumner's scheme by the kind of reaction a breach of the rule produced among those who upheld it. The most sacred rules, mores, were regarded as a conserving force in the life of human beings, protecting what society stands for.

Sumner wrote at a time when the uniformity of nineteenth-century America was coming to an end. In this period of change, conflicts among people of different nationalities and races were emerging from the sameness of small-town America. In writing about and from the vantage-point of an age already gone by, Sumner could be confident that those who made up that passing society stood shoulder to shoulder in agreement on what was most important to preserve. If there was not general consensus on the basic goals of the society, the propriety of the moral order, and the need for all good people to uphold it, to Sumner at least there appeared to be.

Today it is generally recognized that we live in a world of conflict. Consensus on the basic goals of society no longer exists, and debate over what those goals should be has become an important factor in American life. Just as there is less than total agreement on what are the deeply held values of today's members of society, so there is some disagreement as to what is deviant and what is conforming behavior. At the same time, there is probably a deeply held and widely shared view of the expectations in everyday life (how to shake hands, for example, and when and with whom) and also on what constitutes the most deviant and criminal acts (rape, for example). These two definitions of everyday expectations and the most criminal acts are interlocked. The minor social expressions of civility that people offer to one another provide some security at a time when many are shocked and outraged by acts of mugging, rape, and torture of seemingly unprovocative victims. There is consensus that these acts are wrong, although not on how to provide protection or deterrence or on how to punish or rehabilitate offenders.

But in this time of reconsideration of the "old verities," the nature of membership remains sacred. People still want to belong to something; they still want recognition; they still want to be somebody, not in the sense of achievement (although they want this too) but in the sense of belonging. Without membership (and nonmembership as well) there would be no society, only aggregates of human beings who would not be able to create rules or enforce them. Norms go further than protecting, and sometimes threatening, the individual and society; they actually protect members by providing security and cohesion.

What is membership? It refers in the first instance to belonging to an ongoing group that shares a common culture and in which there is a strongly held sense of identification and a great deal of direct affiliation. Further, it is sometimes derived from the personal qualities of the members, as in a family or a friendship clique. But it is much broader than that: ideally, membership is based on a good fit between a person and what is expected of him; between the person's location in the social order and his actions; between the stratum from which he comes and other strata. Finally, membership, on a personal level, has to do with the kinds of claims one person can make on another; it has to do with what you can count on from others and what others will ask of you. All these points are illustrated by being a member of the faculty or student body: there are expectations, prescriptions and proscriptions, a relationship between what one is a member of and the actions that are allowed and forbidden. Students can make claims on other students that they cannot make on teachers, and the reverse is also true. And a member of each group can make demands on the other that would not be made on a colleague or fellow-student.

Norms and Coordination

Many of the norms that govern our behavior in everyday life are conventions, which are taken for granted by members of society. Sumner called these norms folkways because they were not critical for the continuation of the society, were not deeply held by the members, and yet were the ways of ordinary folk. These rules make it possible for people *not* to have to make a decision every day on how to treat one another. Often these rules promote avoidance of getting to know others better, avoidance of conflict, and avoidance of claims made upon others. When students enter a classroom, for example, even for the first time, they know that they are to take seats that have been set aside specifically for them, not the one behind the desk, which is for the teacher. At a funeral, one may smile at greeting a friend or relative whom one has not seen for a long time, but one may not laugh joyfully. One covers his mouth when yawning or coughing, acknowledges with a blessing that someone has sneezed, and ignores the transgression of an adult who fails to do these things but is permitted to correct or reprimand a child.

People are coordinated or are kept in line, both literally and figuratively, by these routine activities. Literally, there are lines waiting to make purchases at a supermarket, to enter a theater, to mount a bus, as well as lines of soldiers or schoolchildren on parade. There is order in these lines and progress toward a goal that is common to all those cooperating. But in a symbolic sense, these events can be seen as similar to the cooperative effort of human beings who are involved with one another, in other types of situations, by chance or by design, for a few fleeting moments or continually over a period of years. The way people act as they drive their cars, sit in a subway, walk into a store, sit at table with members of the family, make or avoid eye contact on the street, ask questions in a classroom—all are part of a scheme in which it can be said that they are "in line" in the sense that they are cooperating by obeying a set of rules.

Keeping people in line is not just a job for ushers or policemen; it is something we do to one another every single day. The line that is kept is not only literal or figurative; it is a kind of social geometry in which there is a fit between the role a person performs and the self he presents in the performance of that role. As a foremost student of contemporary social behavior, Erving Goffman (1967), tells us, a "line" is the stance taken by a person in the performance of a given social role. In such a stance, for example, a person may attempt to appear tough or accommodating, depending on the line he wants to take as he sizes up a situation. Sometimes that line is supported by others and its appropriateness is confirmed by these others in face-to-face interaction. At other times, however, the line is regarded by some as a challenge to the membership of a particular gathering or group, and others seek to disconfirm the identity projected by a person. For example, a student may be told by fellow students that he is showing off in class by asking questions or answering them; or he may be commended by those students for raising questions that result in clarification of classroom material. The first would be a line-challenging response, the second a line-sustaining one.

There is a kind of give and take in projecting and protecting a line, despite the general presence of rules that anticipate the identity of persons with whom we expect to come into contact during the course of the day. These rules provide us with models of responses—to others by ourselves and, alternatively, to us by others. Typically these rules also include a set of personal characteristics we expect others to possess. We expect those we know personally to be much the same from one time to another. We also expect, for example, that a rabbi will be Caucasian, but we would not be surprised to meet a minister or a priest who was black. We would not be surprised if the rabbi introduced us to his wife, but we would be perplexed if the priest did the same thing. Nor would we be surprised if the minister introduced us to his spouse, but what if the minister were a woman and the spouse her husband? In some denominations this would occasion great astonishment, in others very little at all, and both might have expressed astonishment a few years earlier. In other words, membership in a particular category or status carries with it a socially assigned identity, although this is subject to the ebb and flow of social change. If that identity differs in some way from what we anticipate, the rules of identity are violated.

The same may be said about the presence of certain persons on some social occasions. For example, the presence of children at funerals is regarded as inappropriate by those who believe that children do not fit the role of mourner, no matter how close they were to the deceased person. The eighteen-year-old niece of the deceased would be permitted to attend the funeral, but the five-year-old nephew would not. Consider also the endless jokes about relatives, usually the bride's mother, who accompany a newlywed couple on their honeymoon, a clear violation of the rules concerning who is to be present on that occasion; the nature of the violation is made explicit by treating the matter as humor. Much of the humor in the Marx brothers films stems from situations in which they are uninvited guests or secret lovers hiding under the bed when the husband comes home. Charlie Chaplin, on the other hand, was always looking in on the happenings of others rather than crashing their activities. Chaplin was always an outsider who recognized his own inappropriateness in closed groups; the Marx brothers were the more pushy outsiders, who came in uninvited and then complained about the party!

Rules of behavior are pervasive. Man is seldom confronted with a situation in which there are no guidelines for activity, no precedents to be followed, no social expectations of what is appropriate. In fact, there are rules about what to do when the rules of identity are violated, ranging from the silent treatment or the deliberate effort to ignore a minor transgression to expulsion, reprisal, and other forms of punishment. In other words, there are rules for rulebreakers, and there are expected and appropriate behaviors for those who meet them, even suddenly and without preparation. Further, activity that is conforming, socially desired, and rewarded does not automatically lead to bliss. One can be a conformist and still fail to succeed in certain endeavors.

How can that be? Well, there is no simple correlation between the way things are supposed to be and the way things happen. "Life isn't fair," the late President Kennedy is supposed to have said, and he and his family certainly had their share of both good and bad luck. A comment of this kind is a rule in itself; it tells the listener not to question the rules themselves but to attribute failure and other calamities to something outside the rules and beyond the control of human beings. Belief in fate, fortune, luck, and a great variety of religious tenets makes it possible for some people who follow the rules and are nevertheless punished (or not rewarded) to continue to have faith in social norms. If all those who abide by appropriate and proper rules of conduct but

nonetheless come to suffer were to lose faith and turn into antisocial beings, the result would be a world of chaos.

Following the rules involves a great deal of trust on the part
of the upright members of society. Trust is a necessary ingredient
for organized social life. Accordingly, the person who deliberately seeks to violate these standards knows how much trust is
involved to make his rule-violating action possible. To continue
to sustain the trust that is the very essence of social expectations,
it is necessary not only to explain away the person who breaks the
rules but also to honor the often unrewarded virtue of those who
do not. The common man of society who endures the wheeling
and dealing of others and does not complain, at least not too
noisily, was recently exemplified by the former director of the
Federal Bureau of Investigation, L. Patrick Gray, a man who was
still following the rules when everyone around him in the Watergate conspiracy was telling him loud and clear (but not in so many
words) that he had to fudge the investigation of the notorious
break-in.

Not only are there sets of rules about membership and how to
maintain belief in membership through common activities in various collectivities in society; there are also rules that attempt to
regulate the many-faceted relationships among these various collectivities. These are often found under the general category of
law, but they go beyond the law to deal with relationships that are
not recognized in a legal sense. American law, for example, does
not take cognizance of the existence of discrete social classes; yet
the law may be regarded as the regulator and protector of property rights, and it limits access to goods and services for some
groups in the name of preserving such rights. These norms protect established relationships among the various strata and com-
peting groups in American society. When a dominant group's
position in society is questioned, these norms are usually invoked
to secure the claim of that group and downgrade the claims of
others. After the American Civil War, for example, when there
was an opportunity to provide a secure economic base for the
newly freed slaves by confiscating the huge land holdings of
Confederate aristocrats, Congress did not take this action for fear
of setting a precedent concerning the way in which property was
to be treated in American society; even the property of persons

who were legally convicted as traitors was not to be redistributed without compensation. Thus, some oppression in the form of exploitation remained uncompensated in order to protect more sacred norms concerning private property. Reactions to those who violate the rules as well as to the victims of such violations can therefore be seen to involve careful selection of appropriate targets.

Deviance

Given all these norms and normatively oriented behaviors, why are there so many violations, on the one hand, and so many of what Robin Williams (1960) has called patterned evasions of socially recognized rules of conduct, on the other? According to some writers, such as Howard Becker (1963), it is the rules that make violation or the deviance; if there were no rules, there would be no rule-breakers. Thus one starts with an elementary and self-evident statement: All societies have rules, formal or informal, explicit or implicit, for the behavior of their members, and all societies enforce these rules by a variety of rewards for the vast numbers who uphold them and punishments for those who violate them.

From this it might appear that we could define "a deviant" as one who breaks a socially imposed rule, but even as a starting point this definition offers difficulties for sociological analysis. It might be better, as Albert Cohen (1966), Edwin Schur (1971), and many others have suggested, to limit deviance to the violation of rules when such violation incites anger, hostility, resentment, scorn, ridicule, or punitive action in a significant sector of the populace. Jaywalking, then, would not be a deviant act, nor would the failure of a professor to hand in his students' grades on time. However, the former act might become deviant if there were a successful campaign by autoists, parents, and civic groups to arouse the public, just as the latter might similarly be transformed if it were part of a pattern of contempt for the regulations of the institution shown by the particular professor, and if he were reacted to with sufficient hostility by students and administrators.

The breaking of a rule or the failure to fulfill an expectation is generally considered deviance or deviant behavior, although as we shall see, some deviance involves no active rule-breaking at all, and some rule-breaking is difficult to conceptualize as deviant. Special attention will have to be paid to ways of defining social deviance and spelling out its various characteristics. It is far easier to locate and define norms without looking at human interaction than it is to locate and define deviance and deviants; yet both are part of and outcomes of very dynamic social processes.

The fact is that norms reveal what should be, as defined in a given time and place, but not what is or might be. The study of norms raises questions about why people create them and what they expect from their creations; it also raises questions about why people violate norms and how these violations are handled.

Human behavior may be described as norm-oriented behavior, but not all human behavior is normative. Societies are hardly utopias—and it is doubtful that they would be even if everyone followed all the rules. But human beings are adaptive creatures, and both the making of and their violation of norms constitute highly adaptive modes of social living.

NORMS AND SOCIAL LIFE

If human beings can be characterized as capable of treating their own actions reflexively, why are norms made explicit and overt? Surely the fully socialized individual who is aware of his own actions can predict the consequences of any course of action he might follow. Why, then, do people initiate rules?

Human behavior is social behavior insofar as it takes the existence of other people into account. Rule-making behavior is social behavior because it takes into account the context under which the rules will operate. Moreover, rules are initiated because there is some belief that they will deal with a situation in which problems have arisen. They are created to bring about some desired state or outcome. The generating of norms occurs in yet another context: it is an effort to make more predictable and controllable what others might do on a day-to-day basis. The creation of social certainty is a necessary feature of organized social life and promotes that condition.

The first line of predictability occurs in relationships with those with whom we interact in face-to-face association—the people we live and work with in our daily round of life. Such people become very predictable to us. We know not only what time they will arrive at work, or home from work, but also what words they will speak and what facial expressions they will make. A spouse may know immediately that "something is wrong" when his or her mate does not act in the usual way. Occasional changes in behavior require minor adjustments in response, but permanent changes may involve major realignments in a long-standing relationship. Unexpected changes may produce conflict between two people with very strong ties to each other, thereby jeopardizing the relationship. The source of the conflict may be strains in other relationships, as when a wage-earner loses his job and feels less able to command respect from his family, perhaps upsetting the established authority structure between parent and child. Conflict may arise from within a relationship, as when one partner's psychological needs are unrecognized or dealt with inappropriately.

The close contact and erotic attraction between parents and growing child can result in incest and are avoided not just through the famous taboo but also through rules which parents establish concerning dress, physical contact, and flirtatious behavior. Since the relationship between parents and child is important to maintain, both from the society's need to provide protection for its immature members and from the parents' need to fulfill their sense of competency as parents, new rules can be created to take into account the emotional and physical changes in the child. As a child grows older and becomes more aware of its development and its own erotic feelings toward its parents, parents may create rules that restrict the child's access to their bedroom at those times when they are dressing or undressing. Similarly, the child may begin to create its own rules to maintain privacy as a way of receiving validation from others that it is older. Thus the adolescent often insists that parents knock on the door to the room before entering or will post elaborate "Do Not Enter" signs to deter entrance.

Sometimes relationships change because there are new participants performing roles once performed by others, as when a divorced parent remarries. This may create difficulties for children and adults alike, and the creation of new rules may ease the transition into the new situation. Norms, Gouldner (1954) has suggested, are forms of communication that make continuity possible in what may be a problematic situation. When people work closely together for several years, they develop implicit expectations concerning their mutual rights and obligations. Even though the broader purposes of their work may be established by other units in the organization, the members of this small work community feel that their activity is self-directed. They may resent directives from those who set the goals for their organization as a whole, and direct conflict may result.

Chester Barnard (1938) suggests that the good executive never issues an order that he thinks will not be obeyed. One way of maintaining one's authority is to appear not to be issuing orders. On the assembly line, workers do not have to have direct orders from the foreman because the belt brings the work to their stations, freeing the foreman to provide advice and other forms of supervision. Personnel manuals provide information on general rules, such as when workers are to arrive for work, leave for the day, and take coffee breaks. Many norms are made formal and explicit so that people do not have to create and issue them anew every day or have to receive them in this way. Rules spell out in advance what is permissible and what is not. Those with the authority to command can carry out an assignment without appearing to be very bossy or directive. The written rule makes impersonal and thereby softens the demands made upon people, enabling them to consider themselves in control of their own fate.

If norms are created in anticipation of patterned evasion of the norms, then those who conduct enforcement can do so from a strong position, appearing to be reasonable in exercising authority, rather than arbitrary and capricious. Formality and explicitness provide another advantage to those who are expected to enforce rules: They do not have to go "by the book" and enforce each rule but may use discretion in selective enforcement so as to create loyalties among subordinates. In many offices, personnel are traditionally allowed to leave an hour earlier on Fridays. A supervisor has the right to keep his subordinates at their desk until five P.M., but this kind of rigidity would be resented. Workers might engage in sabotage or evade other, more important rules. Flexibility in enforcement creates opportunities to secure greater cooperation on other matters when effort is needed, such as remaining late to complete an assignment without receiving extra compensation.

Many people who have little decision-making power in an organization do not strongly identify with the organization. Much of the work involved at the lower levels of organizations requires little commitment. Formal norms specify the minimal standards of performance and permit the performer to do the job and yet preserve an image of himself independent of the job performed. When the expectations are explicit and easily met, holders of these positions believe that there are compensations for doing a job that they would rather not do.

Many corporations have come to regard workers' loyalty and faithful compliance with the norms as more important than the heroic virtues of craftsmanship and creativity. Consequently, the reward system is based on minimal standards of performance and maximal standards of conformity. Testimonial dinners, watches, pins, and other extrinsic rewards are usual as compensation for deadend jobs. While genuine and supportive communities exist on the job in relatively self-contained work units, employers often try to create loyalty to the corporation itself by such devices as company or plant newspapers, picnics, softball teams, and the like.

Conditions Leading to Noncompliance

The initiation of norms tells much about the tensions and conflicts that exist within groups and organizations. But the mere fact that a rule is created does not mean that there will be instant or widespread obedience. There are several aspects of social life that interfere with compliance, arising out of the uniform patterns of conduct of social life and the context in which the norms are set forth.

First, a rule may not be understood by those who are expected to comply. An invited guest may be expected to arrive at a given time and place, but the directions given him are ambiguous and the time is not specified precisely. Perhaps the would-be host is told that the person will be around to see him in the evening, but "evening" turns out to be four P.M., some three or four hours earlier than expected. In New England, when a person says, "I'll see you later," this remark is the equivalent of "goodby," but elsewhere in America it may express an expectation or even an understanding of an early and specified encounter. Teachers expect students in college to do take-home examinations but may then become incensed when students collaborate on answers, not having made it explicit that this was not permitted.

Second, compliance may not be possible because the person lacks the resources to meet the expectations and demands made on him. On the telephone, the caller asks that a message be taken, but the person on the other end may be a child, a mildly retarded adult, or someone who speaks only a foreign language, and hence is unable to carry out a simple request. A pilot may receive instructions to accept the demands made by a hijacker, including travel to any named destination, but he may be unable to obey the company rule because he lacks the necessary fuel. Parents may expect that their children should be toilet-trained at an age when they are not developmentally prepared to inhibit the need for evacuation.

Third, rules sometimes appear to be irrational. No-smoking signs in college classrooms are generally ignored by students and instructors because they seem to be inspired by what is considered excessive concern for safety where the likelihood of fire is very remote. On the other hand, the no-smoking rule may be observed more strictly in other parts of the college, such as in an art studio or paint storeroom, where the danger of fire is greater. Sometimes rules are rational but the explanation provided for them is not. When a college student, one of the authors was subjected to harassment by security guards who insisted that no more than four people were permitted to sit at any one cafeteria table. The guards offered no explanation for this rule, and the students found their behavior very arbitrary. Eventually, the Dean of Student Life mentioned that the rule had to do with a recent visit from Fire Department inspectors, who were concerned about blockage of aisles in case of the need for emergency evacuation of the area.

Fourth, the likelihood of enforcement also affects compliance with the rules. Notice how carefully drivers come to a full stop at signs of flashing red lights when an officer of the law is visible. Similarly, low rates of absenteeism are found in workplaces on paydays or in classrooms when term papers are to be returned to students, although failure to appear on the particular day would only result in the apparently minor inconvenience of postponing the receipt of check or paper to a near future date, not a severe handicap to some, at least. Parking rules on campuses are selectively enforced, and students may not be permitted to graduate or to reregister for the next semester if they do not pay their fines, but faculty are rarely punished for illegal parking: they know that they can transgress with impunity. The same power of enforcement also obtains with regard to library transgressions, such as fines for late books. People size up a situation, determining the likelihood that they will be apprehended and, if so, subjected to punishment.

Fifth, an order may not receive compliance if it is not in line with a deeply held belief or principle about the nature of authority. The resignations of Elliot Richardson and William Ruckelshaus at the well-known "Saturday Night Massacre" at the Department of Justice is a good example of noncompliance on the basis of belief. The attorney general did not claim that President Nixon was not within his legal right to order the firing of the Special Watergate Prosecutor, Archibald Cox, but Richardson and his associate felt that it was improper of the President to do so and refused to carry out the order. The resistance of the Danish people during World War II to the Nazi orders that they round up all Jews for internment and extermination was based on their strong commitment to belief in citizenship for all, the use of the state to protect human life, and their own autonomy as a nation. Many Danes risked their lives to transport Jews to neutral Sweden and elsewhere.

Finally, the norm may be issued through a channel that is not regarded as legitimate—that is, having the right to issue an order —or it may exceed the perceived authority vested in the person issuing it. The bill of impeachment drawn up by the House Judiciary Committee included many counts based on Nixon's improper use of his office to punish those he saw as his enemies. Even in face-to-face interaction, the authority to issue orders may be challenged. A friend may become affronted when told that he has overstayed his welcome. During an emergency situation, a civilian who directs traffic may be ignored by drivers who regard his presence and directive as having no legal basis.

The study of norms raises many questions about the sociological meaning of human behavior, particularly where the causes and consequences of norms and their violation are concerned. Violations of norms occur in all societies, or at least all modern ones, and constitute a major part of social life. Sometimes the noncompliance is encouraged, often it is ignored, on occasion prevented, and in many instances controlled.

It may be that each society gets the deviance it deserves, but each individual victim (and there are victims in many instances) certainly does not. Further, the deviance a society gets it does not have to have. In the study of norms, sociologists are concerned with both what is and what is possible; with the way things are done and with the various methods available to get them done. A study of norms can provide a view of the quality of life in a society, the mechanisms for generating support for its values in the populace, and its potential for fulfillment of the needs of its members.

2

Deviance

DEFINING DEVIANCE

That rules, important and trivial, are violated with considerable frequency and by large numbers of people should be apparent to any adult in a modern society. In a broad sense, one can speak of violations of the generally accepted rules of behavior in a society as being deviant. In a very technical sense, the violations can be called nonnormative (as distinct from abnormal) behavior. Although *nonnormative* has a more neutral flavor, free of the connotation of condemnation, wrongfulness, or sin that surrounds the word *deviant,* the latter is the more commonly used term in sociology. "Deviant" is not used in a pejorative sense by the sociologist; to identify a form of conduct or a type of person as deviant does not mean that he disapproves of either. In fact, he may very well approve of the behavior or the person, but recognize that it (or he) is widely disvalued in the society. An example would be the defense or espousal of interracial marriage, an unpopular political creed, or the position that all restrictions on the distribution of pornography should be lifted. The social scientist might well study these phenomena as examples of deviance and at the same time find them not only defensible but, from the point of view of his own values, socially and morally correct and desirable.

Furthermore, the term *deviant* is not used in sociology in the numerical sense, to refer to a small number of people, or less than half the population, or those who depart from the ways of the majority. It is not deviant to be a great concert pianist, although very few people achieve this status. Most people are not journalists, but that does not make journalists deviant. A youth may be a freshman in a school where most of the students are in a higher class; in the sense that his class is lower, it might be termed "inferior," but that does not make his position deviant. Each of these and innumerable other activities, statuses, roles, and membership encompass but a small part of the population. Because the number of persons involved is small (as distinct from such categories as being white, or male, or Christian, or part of a family unit), they are interesting for special study, but the study is not that of people who violated rules or who, for any other reason, are put down, cast out, punished, ostracized, or maltreated in society.

Even the violation of rules does not quite constitute the *sine qua non* of deviance. Some rules are so unimportant, are violated so frequently and with such impunity, that no one takes them seriously as rules. Whether such rules should even exist, or why they exist and are still subject to violation and with what consequences, constitutes a problem in social control. Let it suffice here to state that these violations do not constitute deviance. One refers here to jaywalking and double-parking, or to a student's telling his mother that he has finished his homework when in fact he has not even started it. Nor is it deviant, although it is very definitely illegal, to sign a statement that one intends to reside indefinitely in a state in which it is easy to obtain a divorce when the applicant plans to leave that state forever as soon as the decree is granted. In all these instances, the breaking of the rule does not incite a significant amount of social hostility to warrant the label of deviance.

Sometimes rules are espoused but infractions are deliberately overlooked because of the social consequences of strict enforcement. An employer, for example, may deliberately break his own rules concerning adherence to business during working hours in order to show employees that he can be indulgent. Such actions enhance their loyalty and may have consequences at some later time, when the employer might ask employees to stay late without receiving additional compensation.

Some sociologists, such as Edwin Sutherland (1940), have thought of deviance as primarily a matter of who breaks the rule rather than what rule is broken. This is certainly a valuable dimension, but it does not always help. It concentrates on power, on the fact that white-collar criminality generally does not confer the same degree of stigma or social hostility as the criminal behavior of ordinary or lower-class people. It is true, as Charles Winick (1961) showed, that physician narcotic addicts are not treated as junkies in the same way that slum residents are: that celebrities can have illegitimate children (even twins!) without falling into disgrace while one's next-door neighbor in this circumstance has to change her place of residence and take on a mythical status of divorcee or widow; and that even an act so greatly condemned as exhibitionism in front of strange children may be treated with compassion if the transgressor is a man of social standing but meets with outrage if he is not. Bizarre behavior that involves several people, such as "streaking," seems to produce humorous tolerance rather than outrage. The loner is more suspect than the man with friends and family.

But these examples appear to tell only part of the story, although it is an important part. The rich, the celebrated, the powerful are often treated with kindness, compassion, forgiveness, and sympathy for the same acts that incite wrath when committed by others; at times they have even literally gotten away with murder. Nevertheless, they are looked upon with considerable contempt if it is believed, suspected, or known that they engage in pimping or, in some circles, homosexuality, if they are extremely obese or stutter badly, or if they are rumored to be impotent, to cite only a few examples.

A second problem, and one to which we shall return, concerns the question of the public identification of the individual. Obviously, if obesity is defined as a deviant state, there is no problem of visibility. Only by becoming a recluse can one hide this condition (and then one becomes deviant because one is a recluse). But if a couple is into swinging and this is not known to their children, close friends, or neighbors but only to those with whom they perform their activities, then they have not been identified and thus may avoid the wrath of society or its official agencies. Some would say that these people are norm-violators but not deviants, because their violations are not known.

Erving Goffman (1963) who prefers to speak of *stigma* rather than *deviance,* handles this problem by dividing stigmatized persons into two groups: the discredited and the discreditable. In the former category are those who have some characteristic or trait that either is visible or has been made public and that places a disvaluation upon such persons. In the latter category are others who have a trait that would likewise make them disvalued if the characteristic were known, but it is not. Discreditables can be thought of as secret deviants, and it is an interesting problem for sociological study to determine how and why their secret is maintained, who knows and who does not, the niceties and etiquette governing the frequently known but unmentionable, and so on.

This book is about norms and rules, and the violation of these norms and rules. The violators are called deviants. Yet, some examples are included that do not seem to fit: some disvalued persons have broken no rule but are nevertheless studied as if they were deviants, such as stutterers, the obese, albinos, and perhaps the blind, the crippled, the deaf-mute. And if we are going to discuss the stigmatized, we cannot ignore the racially and ethnically branded, those whom Goffman conceptualizes under the heading of "tribal stigma." In this sense, we are talking about something broader than violation of the norms of a society; we are discussing the entire field of people who are regarded negatively, some for having violated such rules, others just for being the sort of people they are or having traits that are not highly valued. No matter what the origin of the disvalued behavior or characteristics, actors must take these definitions into account when interacting with others.

This conclusion raises still another problem when one speaks of deviance. Who is doing the valuation? There are some matters on which society achieves a consensus (no one defends or accepts drunken driving, public urination, forcible rape, or shoving an old lady in order to get a seat on a bus); there are many other matters, large or small in their consequences, on which no consensus can be reached. Some people engage in sexual behavior that others consider outrageous, or appear in public dressed in a manner that is highly disdained by others.

In discussing norm violation, one must ask whether it is a violation that is condemned by all or many; whether some people are favorable to the violation or merely indifferent; whether those who condemn the act are a cultural and political power elite who can easily impose their view on others (as an administrator on a student); whether differences in response to an act correspond to a division along ethnic, class, age, gender, geographic, occupational, or other socially differentiated lines, or whether they are random in the population.

Violation applies to the breaking of rules, usually deliberate and willful but not necessarily so. Because of the consequences for all members of the society, sociologists pay special attention to such transgressions when they are of sufficient significance to provoke a negative reaction or a negative view of the transgressor if the act is known and comes to the attention of the public. In this sense, it may be a violation of the rules of a school to cut classes, but to do so is not to commit a deviant act, although the act might well be turned into deviance if the students, professors, parents, and administrators were sufficiently incensed about it.

Let us look at a few lists of people whom various sociologists include when they use the term deviant. Fred Davis (1961), deeply involved in work on polio victims, wrote that under *deviant* he would include the racially stigmatized, career women, such disvalued radicals as Communists, criminals, the physically handicapped, the mentally ill, and homosexuals, among many others. For Davis, they were all deviants, "albeit," he hastened to add, "in different ways and with markedly different consequences for their life careers." This was in 1961; perhaps a decade or more later, Davis might have revised this list.

A few years later, in 1966, Albert Cohen spoke of deviance as involving knavery, skulduggery, cheating, unfairness—and the list could be continued, but one can gather the thrust of Cohen's thinking from these few items.

But Cohen is saying that unfairness, for example, is deviant, not that everyone who commits an unfair act is a deviant person. For who among us has never been unfair to another? Whether to call the perpetrator of a deviant act a deviant may depend on the seriousness of the offense and the pattern of activities of the alleged offender.

Others have written of deviance and deviants as a job or career, including stripteasers and topless barmaids, masseuses and their clients in parlors where the message of the massage is indubitably sexual, and the like. What we have here, when we combine these several lists, are primarily two types of people: those who have violated a rule, and those who have not but are nevertheless part of an outcast group. Judith Lorber (1967) has called the latter "accidental deviants." We prefer to see them as "involuntary deviants." By this we do not mean that the prostitute voluntarily wishes to be seen with hostility and to be labeled deviant but only that the status that earns her the label is one she entered rather voluntarily and was not the result of ethnicity, a birth defect, an illness, or an accident.

Does it make sense from the viewpoint of sociological study to place such a wide variety of persons into a single category? Apparently it does, if we are looking at how society reacts to and treats people who come to be seen as disvalued, what the consequences of this social hostility are, and how persons who are the objects of such hostility cope with life. In this sense, the single category is useful. But this does not mean that all those placed within it have been evaluated by the social scientist with accuracy. It is possible that in 1961 there were observers who would have denied that career women were disvalued or that they were violating any of the written or unwritten rules by which American women were supposed to live or that they belonged to anything remotely resembling an outcast group. This would be a matter of taking issue with how Fred Davis saw society at the time, but not with the basic theme of his presentation.

However, there is another perspective, one that would concentrate on the rules of society, formal and informal, explicit and implicit. Some would maintain that a proper and unified area of study must exclude those who have broken no rule, even though they are indubitably outcast. There is no right or wrong in this;

it is a matter of the relative usefulness of one perspective over another. In this book, we seek to balance the two approaches, to concentrate on the rules and rule violations, on the one hand, and, on the other, on the stigma applied to those who have violated these rules and also to people who are handicapped or for some other reason are victimized by a hostile and outcasting society. The two themes merge as one notes the similarity of the hostile reactions as well as the mechanisms used by the recipients of hostility to cope with life under conditions of adversity. But the themes diverge as one looks at the origins of the deviance (on the part of the victim or the transgressor) and at social policy for the handling of such persons on the part of cultural and political leaders.

The lists of those who are considered deviant are not definitions in themselves but may give rise to a definition. People or things are placed within a group because they have elements of similarity, despite the fact that they are dissimilar in an infinite number of ways. Then, when one looks at all the examples within a category, the boundaries of the category can be expressed in general terms. Or the process may work in the reverse manner: the general definition makes it possible to choose individual instances that fall within the boundaries. From the lists, one sees that it does not work simply to make deviance synonymous with rule violation, for this excludes the retardate and the polio victim, and it includes those who violate rules so trivial that little or no attention is paid to the transgression. The key to knowing that deviance exists is to note how members of society react to some individuals, statuses, and groups. This is not to say that the reactors, the "good" and "upright" and "normative" members, *create* deviance by their hostile reaction. It is merely to say that the hostile reaction is the feature that makes it known to the sociologist that the person or behavior is deviant. In other words, the subject of study is people who, because of what they do or what they are, or of what they are blamed for doing or suspected of being, are treated by society in a manner less favorable than are others.

Numerous definitions have been offered to cover this phenomenon. We select one that may be a little complex at first glance (and we will make it even more complex) but one that appears to us to encompass the necessary features of this area of study. According to Edwin Schur (1971:24):

> human behavior is deviant *to the extent that* it comes to be viewed as involving a *personally discreditable* departure from a· group's normative expectations, *and it elicits* interpersonal or collective reactions that serve to "isolate," "treat," "correct," or "punish" individuals engaged in such behavior. (Emphasis in the original.)

If one wishes to make this definition more precise, one might expand it to *human beings* as well as human behavior, so as to include those whose deviance comes from what they are and not from what they do, Lepers, for example, may elicit the types of reaction that Schur spells out for conduct. We would also add, to cover the fact that some socially condemned behavior, because of secrecy, never comes to elicit these interpersonal and collective reactions, that the behavior would elicit them *if it came to be known.*

It is difficult to locate a single word that covers all the persons and behavior that are usually encompassed by this theme, but we believe that the concept of *disvalued* persons and behavior is as close to it as any. While the study of norms focuses on all of the rules and guidelines for behavior in a society, the study of deviance concerns not all rule violations but only those that are disvalued. This appears to capture what sociologists have included under the rubrics of *nonnormative behavior, stigma,* and, to a certain extent, as a special aspect of rule-breaking, *crime.*

THE DIMENSIONS OF DEVIANCE

Sometimes it is said that rules are made to be broken. If this means that the purpose of making the rule is so that someone can violate it, the statement is hardly true. But if one interprets the remark to mean that no social rule exists that is not broken, the truth is apparent. Even when mores are particularly strong, such as the prohibition against cannibalism and mother-son incest, violations are not unknown. Yet the manner in which we conform to most rules is very much like the way we breathe or eat: it

appears "natural" to do things as they are supposed to be done,
and this is often accomplished in an unthinking, reflexive, un-
doubting manner—what sociologists call the taken-for-granted
world. Nevertheless, rules *are* disobeyed, sometimes openly but
perhaps more often secretly, sometimes unknowingly but usually
quite deliberately; they are also made so that they can be bent,
twisted, circumvented, obeyed in letter but not in spirit or even
the reverse, and in other ways flouted to a limited extent or with
sufficient mitigation as to reduce the strength and degree of the
anticipated social sanction for violation. Thus, failure to conform
to a norm is not a yes/no, either/or matter. In fact, even when
laws are involved, there are circumstances when it is impossible
to make a clear-cut statement that the law was or was not violated;
when rules far less explicit than the written laws are concerned,
certainty cannot always be attained.

The social scientist must first determine what the norms of a
society are in order to investigate whether they are violated, how
frequently, by whom, under what circumstances, and with what
consequences. Merely to identify the norms is not a simple task,
although one can start with the universal assumption that norms
exist in all societies. To determine the legal prescriptions and
proscriptions, particularly in a modern and literate society, appears to be easy. The student need only examine the laws to find
that it is against the law (a rule violation) to commit robbery or
burglary or to marry one's brother or sister. In some countries
it is against the law to fail to vote, and in many countries it is a
crime to organize a political party that challenges the basic precepts of the government. It might appear at first glance that one
either commits such a prohibited act or does not. But leaving
aside for the moment the problem of false accusation, there is
always a need to determine whether what was done did in fact
constitute burglary or robbery or rape, or whether it was indeed
a political party that was organized.

Then, there are many rules in the penal codes that meet little
social support and the violation of which seldom results in prosecution and never in the hostile reaction of large parts of the
populace that is the hallmark of deviance. These may include
some traffic laws, blue laws, white-collar crime such as fee-split-

ting, and income tax violations that can be considered cutting corners rather than out-and-out larceny.

Both for legal purposes, to determine whether a punishment should be accorded and if so, to what degree, and for social purposes, to predict the amount and extent of hostility an act will probably provoke, one must place it in context and look at the actor's motivation and intent and the myriad of surrounding circumstances. The intoxicated hit-and-run driver is subject to greater punishment for being drunk, but for the child molester under the influence of the same amount of alcohol the intoxication reduces the strength of the outrage directed toward him. The simple rule that it is illegal to run a red light has many exceptions, such as police and fire vehicles and ambulances on emergency duty, and the further exception that there may be a policeman on duty who is directing traffic, superseding the mechanical lighting system. Then, these situations aside, just examine the complications of the problem: Was the driver of the vehicle on a bicycle or in an automobile? Was he sober or drunk? Was he rushing a person to a hospital? The possible circumstances that could explain, justify, or excuse the act, at least to an extent, are almost limitless. And if courts do not always take these matters into account (sometimes they do not, for many reasons), family, peers, employers, friends, people we know and those who may learn of our transgressions although not acquainted with us, certainly do. These people, the significant others and the general public or the "generalized other," as George Herbert Mead (1934) called them, have a sort of automatic bookkeeping ledger in which each of us is judged according to the personal standards of the judge, which do not always reflect the standards of the community. Thus, we are seen not as people who do or do not violate the norms but in terms of what norms we violate, how frequently, in what manner, and with what justifications or mitigations.

It is not only on the side of the violation that flexibility and judgment are taking place but on the side of the compliance as well. Sometimes sociologists speak of deviance as the other face of conformity, but *conformity* is a term that suggests slavish conventionality. It might be said that we are expected ideally to conform but not to be conformists. (This is somewhat akin to the fact that the violation of certain relatively unimportant laws can be called crime, but the violators are hardly criminals.) To conform is to comply with the rules, whether of society or of a group with which one is involved. Now, sometimes we may not like these rules, and perhaps we personally did not have much to do with making them. But we inherited them, they are the only norms we know, they have become the taken-for-granted ways of our world, and for the most part we would have a hard time living without these rules. In other instances, we join a group and the act of joining means that we have voluntarily decided to subscribe to or obey the ways of the group. One does not have to go to college, but if one does, there are rules governing registration, courses for which one is or is not eligible, requirements for graduation, and innumerable other ways of behaving that one cannot ignore without jeopardizing his or her right to remain a college student. And this is true even if one thinks that many of these rules are senseless (as they well may be) or unfair.

Yet all of us comply most of the time to most of the rules. It is better if we like the rules, but like them or not, we manage to find out that it is more convenient to live by them than to antagonize people, whether those in authority or friends, family, and peers, by disobeying. But the word *conformity* suggests overcompliance, the unwavering and largely unquestioning following of a leader. If the deviant is the sinner, evil incarnate, the conformist is the Babbitt, the small-town Main Street follower who dares not swerve from the path mapped out for him, and does not have the initiative and creativity to question that path. Ritualistically, he performs exactly as he is expected and asked to perform, and his unwavering loyalty to the way things are is inherently conservative.

Thus society has you coming and going. You are trapped! Do and be damned, don't and you'll get caught and hanged! Is that what the picture adds up to? Not quite. This is more a caricature than a picture, more a parody than a portrait.

The world of social reality is not divided in splendid simplicity between those who obey the rules and those who flout them. There is the overconformist, whose rigidity often provokes ridicule and sarcasm or some other mild manifestation of hostility (except among those who share the rigid ways), and, at the other end, the rebel, sometimes rejecting the norms for the sake of that rejection. But almost all people fall between these extremes.

On the one hand, most human beings follow the rules of their group and at the same time most violate some of these rules from time to time, or at least find ways of circumventing them. Yet to speak of all of us as being deviant in one way or another or to some extent would itself be both an exaggeration and a simplification, for the violators themselves do not fall into a cohesive, easy to classify group.

This brings us to the problem of the dimensions of deviance, a matter we find implicit in Schur's definition, more than in the definitions offered by other sociologists. Schur uses the expression "to the extent that" in describing the probability and severity of social hostility to an act or a person. Some acts provoke far greater hostility than others. The public measures an act informally, usually without calculation; the measurement may be influenced by the press and other media, by gossip, by statements of public officials, by racial and other ethnic prejudices and precommitments, by an ideology that wants to believe things to be a certain way. All of this helps to account for the nature of the reaction.

Sometimes the person is not stigmatized with a deviant identity. In the view of Howard Becker (1963), he does not obtain a master status that is a deviant one. This may be because the act is fleeting or is indulged in under conditions of anonymity (not exactly the same as secrecy, as will be elaborated on later) or because the act is not that important (as, for example, if one believes that another is a bore) or because it does not have continuity or chronicity (letting wind in public is a single act, but having a deviant sexual pattern is generally considered to follow an individual, to become attached to him, to be virtually inescapable) or because it is trivial (as sneezing without covering one's mouth, a one-time act that can hardly be compared to the one-time act of assault upon another person).

If doing the right thing, being a good citizen, complying with the major and some of the minor demands of one's family, peers, and the populace in general can go so far in the direction of overconformity that it becomes a kind of "deviance," the reverse is even more true. The word *straight,* particularly in its nonsexual connotation, can have a pejorative tone, suggesting an ultraconservative morality that does not recognize the needs of a changing society and that is unable or unwilling to bend with it.

Thus violation of norms has dimensions. The .world is not divisible into those who obey and those who violate. And the dimension that sociologists tend to emphasize is the degree to which the violation is likely to provoke hostility, if the act is known. This does not mean that the actor himself has done nothing to bring forth this reaction, that he is the passive and innocent victim of people who have nothing better to do than go around denouncing those unlike themselves. Most rule violation is not of this type. It is, rather, that the degree to which the violation can be considered deviant has only one objective measurement: the nature, extent, degree, universality, certainty, of the hostility—or, as mentioned, of the hostility that could reasonably be anticipated if the act were to become known.

Nature, extent, degree, universality, certainty—are they not all the same thing? Not at all, although there must be some correlation. There are violations that provoke universal but mild hostility: for example, arranging a date between a sixty-year-old woman and a twenty-year-old man. Almost everyone would condemn the cruelty of the practical jokester, but once he was reprimanded, the act could quickly be forgotten. One could speak of this as universality and certainty, but mild in the reaction provoked. An opposite example would be found in the guerrilla or terrorist, seen as a hero by those who identify with his aspirations, and as the worst type of murderer by those who are his enemies. The reaction here is not universal, but whether hostile or approving, it is extremely strong.

There is a tendency to categorize conduct as deviant or normative rather than along a continuum of behavior. Then, having failed to distinguish between the slightly deviant and the very deviant, writers have applied to the former conclusions based on analysis of the latter. Generalizations, theoretical considerations, and proposals for social policy for the mildly deviant may be quite inapplicable to the extreme cases.

Some people are more deviant than others, both in the frequency of the act that earns them this label and in the nature of the act. In the case of crimes, this distinction has been expressed by the division into felonies, misdemeanors, and offenses, or into various groups of felonies categorized according to the severity of the punishment that can be inflicted or (what might be quite a different matter) the nature of the punishment that actually is inflicted on one who is found guilty. For noncriminal deviant acts and violations there is no official bookkeeping, but one can nevertheless gain a feeling for the distinctions by noting the reactions of others.

If the rule in question is not held with the same reverence by all in society, one of the questions that arises is whether the hostility is a reflection of the attitudes of the people who constitute a center of power. On the surface, this involves the rather simple question of whether they can have legislation passed and in other ways make their viewpoint strongly felt in the areas of employment, election or appointment to office, or other societal rewards. Certainly, in the 1960s and even later, abortion and marijuana smoking represented acts that were condemned by only a portion of the population of the United States, but it was the portion that controlled the laws and had the power to enforce its will on the rest of society. It was not quite that simple, however, for the groups in opposition had voices and votes and were challenging their adversaries for power.

In many societies, however, the question is not only one of police, judicial, legislative, and other governmental power; it has even more to do with whether the type of behavior conforms to the "official culture." One does not eat during the minister's sermon in church, certainly not a sandwich, although perhaps a piece of candy can be surreptitiously sucked; this is the "just-not-done" type of behavior that is informally frowned upon. No laws are passed to prohibit such acts; it is common knowledge that they are not to be done and if done, not to be boasted of. Power here seems to consist of the tacit agreement among most people who belong to a society, or to a group within it, about what is right and what is wrong.

A further complication arises when a deviant act is committed by someone from elite society, who, as a consequence, is therefore likely to be exempt from strong informal and formal social sanctions. Speeding, drunken driving, marijuana smoking, the use of other prohibited drugs, the importation and selling of such drugs, having illegitimate children, being "known" (informally, by gossip) as a homosexual—all such behaviors result in only mild reproof or none at all, and sometimes the transgression is even ignored. The societal reaction to the deviant involves both who he is, in terms of social power, and what he has done. This does not mean that the powerful and the wealthy can get away with anything, although sometimes they do. Note that the examples cited here are cases of marginal deviance, where the act does not meet quite universal condemnation and sometimes even receives a bit of social support.

When the group that opposes a certain type of behavior and places the deviant label on it is less than the whole population, there are still further dimensions that must be investigated. Does it consist of a special sector of the populace or is it a representative cross-section? Smoking marijuana in the 1960s was certainly condemned by far fewer college students, working youths of college age, and older persons with higher education than by the rest of the population. In studying a deviant act and determining how deviant it is and in whose eyes, one should ask whether and how strongly it is condemned by different ethnic, racial, sex, and age groups and other portions of the population. More than that, it should be determined whether an act meets social approval or merely indifference among those who do not condemn it. The quality that has come to be known as salience involves the question of how strongly one feels on an issue. Black people are likely to be less condemnatory of ghetto rioting than whites, but they are seldom indifferent to the act, for, by virtue of their own racial identification, the act itself and its consequences concern them. On the other hand, college students who do not smoke pot are likely to take the attitude that they couldn't care less what others do and would probably be hostile to those who condemn such activities.

A Matter of Time and Place

Deviance has a temporal quality to it. Some acts that are condemned at one period are viewed less harshly and are even accepted at another period, and the reverse is also true. Such practices as cohabitation before marriage, divorce, and swearing in the presence of both sexes are much less deviant today in the United States than they formerly were, if they can properly be labeled deviant at all. Not only can a woman have an abortion today but she can acknowledge it publicly—something that would have been impossible in America before 1960. At one time, it was reprehensible for an unmarried son, no matter what his age, to live outside the home of his parents, for a daughter to do so was unthinkable. Later, not only did this behavior become normative, but the son or daughter who was still living "at home" at age 30 came to be ridiculed and considered deviant.

In the 1920s, a man was not permitted on a public bathing beach in and around New York City unless the entire upper part of his body, up to the neck and shoulders, was covered. A shoulder strap on the upper part of the bathing suit (which resembled an undershirt) could be slipped down to the biceps only at the risk of the offender's receiving a summons from a policeman and a fine in court. By the 1970s, few parts of the human anatomy were still left unexposed on these same beaches; to appear today on a beach dressed in the attire deemed proper a half century ago would be considered oddball, eccentric, and would provoke ridicule even to the point of being deviant.

Another example of rapid change in attitudes is found in the significant area of race relations. Before the 1940s, hardly a city or town in the United States was not Jim Crow in its restaurants, hotels, and other public accommodations. For people of different races to eat together was then deviant, and for a "proper" or "decent" restaurant to serve them was unknown. A decade or two later it became deviant to react with overt hostility toward such interracial mingling.

These are but a few illustrations of the point that deviance is not immutable and timeless but grows and diminishes, rises and disappears. Its temporal nature can be exaggerated, however. While public attitudes toward certain forms of disfavored and disvalued behavior may change with regard to the nature of the sanction or the evaluation of the perpetrator, the immediate hostility may persist. Thus, child abuse is always looked upon with hostility, but the accused may be regarded as ill and in need of compassion and rehabilitation, or as criminal and deserving of severe punishment. Furthermore, changes with time should be seen as only one aspect of a larger and much studied issue, namely, that deviance is culturally relativistic. What is disvalued in one society may not be scorned in another, and certainly the extent to which negative sanctions are imposed differs considerably.

This very simple statement has given rise to two problems that cause difficulties for analysis. On the one hand, cultural relativism has been exaggerated. The fact is that there is considerable agreement across cultures and across time on activities that are unacceptable to a populace. On the other hand, it is undeniable that various societies have permitted, institutionalized, and encouraged what most human beings have grown up to condemn. From today's vantage point, should sociologists looking back at American slavery, genocide in Nazi Germany, and the acts committed in the name of colonialism and imperialism say that these forms of behavior were not deviant because they were not condemned by significant portions of the populace in which they were committed?

To answer this question, we must return to the concept of deviance as an area of study. If deviance consists of acts and persons that are not necessarily bad, harmful, and antisocial but *are so defined* by the members of the society in which they take place, it is easy to see that the American slave trade and slaveholding were not deviant. They were, in fact, quite strongly approved by the nation's most powerful forces. This is not to condone them; in fact, one might readily condemn the country in which they took place as normative acts.

Salience and Seriousness

In discussing the seriousness of the violation of norms, Sumner used the distinction between mores and folkways. A further method of distinction is available for transgressions against the laws, or crimes. Unlike socially condemned noncriminal acts, crimes have been officially rated according to the degree to which they are seen as evil. The simplest system of rating uses three categories: felonies, which are the most serious; misdemeanors; and violations or offenses, which are lesser infractions of the law that are often not counted as crimes at all. The distinction between a felony and a misdemeanor involves the degree of punishment that may be meted out to one who is found guilty. At least in the eyes of the lawmakers and those segments of society that give social and political support to them, the category and the seriousness of a crime are measurable, the yardstick being the severity of the punishment. The range of crimes includes those for which death can be imposed, those that can be punished by prison terms, and, lowest on the scale, those punishable only by fines. This is not, however, a continuous system of classifying the degree of "evil" imputed to an act. Corporal punishment, for example, may also be invoked; how, then, can one determine the relative seriousness with which two acts have been conceptualized if the first is punishable by forty lashes and the second by four months in prison?

The major effort to measure the seriousness of criminal acts (particularly delinquent ones committed by young people) and rank them in order of the degree of hostility with which they are generally regarded by upright people was undertaken by Thorsten Sellin and Marvin Wolfgang (1964). Obviously, a similar study might be made of all deviant acts, criminal and noncriminal. Some are more deviant than others. This is a matter of salience and can be quantified only by noting how strongly the acts are condemned by large segments of the population. Evidently, being the father of an illegitimate child is not looked upon with as much disfavor as being the mother; being an effeminate male is viewed with more disfavor than being a mannish woman; smoking marijuana is not so strongly condemned as mainlining heroin; overcharging by a storekeeper is not condemned as much as stealing from a storekeeper; and so on. It is the differences in intensity of condemnation that compel the social scientist to see deviance as a matter of degree. In no instance does grading some acts as less deviant imply that they are morally more justifiable or show better judgment than other acts—that overcharging by a storekeeper, for example, is a less heinous act than stealing from him. What the sociologist is saying here is that, on the basis of research, it is not so regarded by the general public.

The Many Dimensions of Deviance

In sum, the dimensions of deviance would appear to involve the following factors:

How many people see the act negatively, a matter quite different from the more frequently studied problem of how many people break the rule.

Do others see the act positively, or are they indifferent?

Do discrete segments of the population view it differently?

Do those who see it negatively exercise considerable political and police power?

Is the negative view the society's official judgment?

Are there official governmental sanctions for the act?

Does the performer himself see his action as righteous?

Is there social support for the act from others?

How certain is it that the actor, if apprehended, will meet social condemnation?

How strong will this condemnation be?

Deviance, in short, is not a simple matter. Within limits, one can say that an act is criminal or not, although the gray area is a large one, and many court cases have been involved in deciding, not whether a given individual committed the act, but whether, in the circumstances, it constituted a crime. Note, for example, the great lengths to which congressmen, lawyers, and others went in attempting to determine what constituted an impeachable offense, until the question became moot as a result of Richard Nixon's resignation.

For noncriminal deviance and criminal nondeviance, there is no all-or-nothing proposition, no pigeonhole in which to put the act or actor. One cannot merely ask whether or not they are deviant but must ask, rather, how deviant, in whose eyes, and with what consequences.

3

Keeping People in Line

SOCIAL CONTROL

Social control—how members of society keep one another in line—is an aspect of modern sociology that has been attracting increasing scholarly attention. It is a perspective on social life based on many sound assumptions, the main one being that during the course of a day all of us do many things that we would prefer not to do, or resist doing such things although they sorely tempt us. Even the classroom professor is exercising a form of social control—not merely in taking attendance and giving grades but in teaching, particularly in courses on deviance, that the disrespectable elements in society do not have that much fun. Demonstrating the hardships involved in being a criminal, a prostitute, a homosexual, or a vagrant—which is done by mass media and social institutions much more than by professors—may itself be a way of warning against the pitfalls of such activities or careers. It sets the deviant apart from one's own kind and reaffirms the rules for conforming members of society.

Social control operates through law, police, courts, and prisons; it operates through authority figures on whom we are dependent, such as parents; but it is very pervasive on less authoritative

49

and formal levels as well. When people get together and talk
about their absent friends, when they ridicule rivals, or when they
use sarcasm to bring a potentially rebellious member of their
group back into line, they are practicing social control. People
who seek to enforce the rules for members or to draw the boundaries separating members from nonmembers have to maintain a
very delicate balance. When the method used is inappropriate,
perhaps too strong for the transgression noted, one runs the risk
of crystallizing the deviance into an alternative standard of behavior. On the other hand, inaction or a weak or uncertain response may lead to more serious breaches of expected behavior.
The use of inappropriate forms of social control, such as preventive detention or alleged overreaction by police during an alter-
cation, may be regarded by others as itself a violation of the rules.
Many observers consider American laws concerning what have
been characterized as "crimes without victims," such as homosexuality, drug use, and prostitution, as resulting in a general
contempt for law and for enforcement procedures, calling into
question the legitimacy of other laws and the justice of our particular system. Similarly, the Watergate conspiracy involved
some of the highest law-enforcement personnel in the nation,
many of whom in other contexts had raised the cry of "law
and order."

Face-to-Face Interaction

The way in which regulation occurs is evident in even the most
familiar behaviors. When two strangers come into contact in a
public place, each lets the other know that he does not intend to
harm the other and expects that the other has the same attitude.
Strangers generally exhibit what Goffman (1963) calls "civil inattention," following an implicit set of rules concerning physical
distance, appropriate forms of address, and the kinds of questions that may be asked. These rules about social distance are
taken for granted and are often unnoticed until they are violated.
When a stranger approaches us and asks the time we generally
oblige, if possible. The request is appropriate and we think noth-

ing of it, particularly if it is made during the day among lunchtime crowds.

We might become more uneasy about the same request made in a different context, perhaps late at night on a lonely street. Approaching a stranger to ask the time when the public place is deserted may require a special effort to reveal to the other that one's intent is harmless. Crowds regulate behavior in the streets in one way; empty streets require one to be more selective about stopping to answer a stranger's questions. Muggers, of course, know the rules about public behavior as well as the conforming members of society do, and becoming aware of their tactics is an essential part of the armor that people symbolically put on when they use public places at different times of the day.

Strangers generally demonstrate to each other that they do not intend harm by following certain rules that guide social interaction in public places. Notice, for example, how people avoid staring at others on subway trains or buses or, when caught staring, deliberately look away. When one arrives at an elevator, even though another person is already waiting and may be assumed to have summoned the elevator, the newcomer will deliberately push the button, letting everyone present know of his harmless intent. In turn, the first person may clear his throat or smile slightly at the person pressing the button. Interestingly, people who are not used to being in crowds of strangers—for example, mentally retarded adults first released into the community from an isolated institution—may call attention to themselves by staring a great deal. After several months of community living, they are generally able to avoid engaging in behaviors that others in the community may find provocative.

Public order depends on cooperative activity as well as avoidance of dangerous situations. It is important to recognize also that some people are able to get together and establish or maintain relationships despite many contacts with others in public places. While the rules of public order require that strangers provide "civil inattention" to others, people who are friends, relatives, or business associates try to sustain their little social unit in public places, setting themselves apart from others near them. This is accomplished in several ways aimed at preventing incursions from the surrounding social environment. Maintaining interaction in crowded places is a difficult thing to do since strangers are distractions as well as possible sources of interference.

A social unit may be maintained in a public place through the use of objects that symbolize social boundaries, such as books, bags, or clothing. Goffman (1972) refers to such devices used in this way as "markers." This kind of behavior creates a territory which people share temporarily with others and also prevents outsiders from interfering and attempting to use the same space. Conversation itself establishes a kind of membrane around the discussants that excludes potential participants from this temporary social unit. Even when people are disagreeing, they are still involved in a unity of activity that requires cooperation—for example in taking turns when talking, looking at the other, or showing the speaker that one is now playing the role of a listener.

Maintaining the social unit, even if it is a temporary one, is an activity that is respected by the participants. A conversation that starts out innocently discussing business or some other mundane activity may be full of sexual innuendo, but the ambiguity of language permits one party to choose not to recognize the suggestiveness of a remark or to ignore a slip the other makes in speech that reveals some unconscious concern or unresolved problem. Thus the situation can be preserved in spite of the accidental or intentional introduction of these kinds of emotionally meaningful material.

In any encounter a person has to establish a reason for being party to it as well as to act to help maintain it. Even when his reason for being present is not appropriate, he may still be expected to maintain the spirit of the occasion. For example, a guest at a cocktail party who does not drink will be expected not to act judgmentally when others consume alcoholic beverages. Even when a person is not able to establish any right to be present, as when he is a crasher at a party, a simple apology may have to be accompanied by an appropriate display of embarrassment so that everyone present can reaffirm the purpose of the occasion. If such displays are not forthcoming, those with a right to be present might feel it necessary to enforce the rules directly, by ousting the interloper.

The regulation of entry into ongoing temporary social units is very different from the way in which the assumption of membership in permanent groups or organizations may be ceremonialized. The latter represents a special moment set aside from everyday life, and a great deal of attention is paid to the event. Even in everyday social life, there are times when it is made known to outsiders that entry into a temporary social unit is possible or impossible. From a distance, two people standing together may appear to be available for conversation to someone who knows them. Yet when the newcomer is close enough to hear what is being discussed, he may learn that the ongoing encounter is something special and that his presence is unwanted at that moment. He may be able to enter the gathering at a later time, when it is not focused around this important albeit temporary activity. The discussants may indicate this change in the situation by altering their physical position, making themselves more open to outsiders. Again, what may appear to an outsider to be simply a group of people enjoying a sunny day may on closer inspection turn out to be an English class or a developing conspiracy. The forms of expression may be different in face-to-face interaction than in organizations or institutions, but social-control activity is certainly to be found.

Institutions

Social control, involving both informal practices and formal rules, operates in various kinds of ongoing settings. Institutions and organizations provide many examples of how these processes of enforcement work, particularly when new members are introduced into positions or when others are excluded from incumbent positions. Orientation sessions, interviews, introductions, and other ways of introducing people into organizations and institutions provide clear indications to all of the new responsibilities acquired by recruits. Social organizations vary in their need to enforce the norms concerning social solidarity and in their efforts to ceremonialize inductions. Military organizations, in which each member may at some time be required to risk his life for another in battle, ceremonialize the process of becoming a member, mainly through oaths of allegiance, recognition of passage from one status to another, special training that is set apart from the rest of society, and the stripping of rank from those who fail in their duties or are traitors.

The importance of social solidarity and teamwork is an important consideration in every organization, not just those whose members count on each other in an ultimate way. One of the commonsense notions about institutions and organizations is that productivity is measured in easily observed ways. We know, for example, whether a sanitation department is doing a good job by simply determining if the garbage has been picked up or the streets have been cleaned. However, working for others means that some social criteria will also be imposed on the performance of a task, such as the worker's willingness to appear busy on the streets even when the garbage has already been collected. Working with others means that standards having to do with teamwork will emerge and be sustained independently of what supervisors or outsiders say. Work teams often devise a norm for what they consider to be a fair day's work. They may take a long time cleaning up rather than push on with the job simply because working fast might make the slower workers appear to be shirkers when a foreman is present.

Thus the risk of failure in an organization is based not merely on one's inability to meet some objective standard of performance; one's style of working becomes important when significant others are watching. Ways of convincing others that one is working hard are sometimes created, as when office workers pile material onto their desks or bureaucrats stuff their briefcases before a weekend. Rituals are often introduced into seemingly rational organizations as ways of alleviating stress. Regular lunchtime discussions of work may be a way of getting to know how much others are producing and where one stands in comparison to one's peers. There are various publics in any organization, and making their responses manageable and predictable is one of the central activities of all those with fixed assignments in an organization. These instances of anticipating the possible costs of failure to conform are clear examples of how social control operates, not only upon the deviant members of society, but upon the conforming members as well.

Institutions constitute what can be considered an occupational community, in which the worker is judged for his contribution in sustaining the community as well as for his contribution toward achieving its objectives. They are also regarded as the right way to get certain necessary tasks accomplished. By "right" we do not mean the most efficient way to do things but simply what is regarded as legitimate or mandated by society. Once an institution gains a monopoly over a set of tasks, it is expected that all members of society will recognize that the institution possesses knowledge concerning the one best way of accomplishing these tasks.

Religious organizations provide an interesting example of how institutions seek to regulate access to alternative ways of solving human problems. The Catholic Church has been able to absorb many potential sources of fission within it by establishing saint-hoods and encouraging those with strong religious callings to enter monastic life, where they can devote themselves to a life of good work for the benefit of all mankind, under the direction of the church. In a more mundane way, the medical profession provides another example. It has discouraged competitive methods of providing health care—for example, by claiming that osteopaths and chiropractors are charlatans and quacks. When the medical profession found that it could not prevent people from using these services or keep potential recruits from learning how to perform them, it became interested in supervising the application of these treatments. Thus it maintained its domination of medicine in the area of health care.

Once the legitimacy of an institution is established as the primary provider of important services, as in matters of life and death, criminality, or safety, it is able to control those who will be allowed to perform these tasks. The professions routinely handle other people's emergencies, dominating relationship with clients and with subordinate occupational groups; they have gained control over their work environment and the requirements of entry into their fields; they have established ways of categorizing the problematic aspects of daily life and routine procedures for dealing with them. The professions have convinced society at large that they are capable of coping with the uncertainties of living. In an industrial society, which is based on a highly refined division of labor, they perform many social-control activities by determining who is capable of working, who may own what property, what the contractual obligations between consumers and suppliers or between management and labor are, and how to build transportation networks or edifices that permit safe and easy access.

The Medical Profession: A Case History

The professions have a societal mandate to provide help for people in different areas of need—for example, where there are problems of legality, health, housing, and civic planning. These are areas laymen know little about, and as a result they extend trust to a profession. Much of what professional practice consists of is indeed mysterious to laymen, and few of us are capable of evaluating the professional help we receive. How does a profession regulate itself so that it can maintain the confidence of the general public? The area of medical practice provides an illustration of how social control ensures a minimal standard of competency.

First, the formal criteria for entrance to a medical school exclude most of the applicants, and those who are accepted as students by the medical community regard themselves as lucky. Many medical students come from families in which one or more members are physicians, and they are highly motivated to succeed in their training and somewhat prepared to face the rigors of medical school. Anticipation of membership in this occupational community, even when they are still undergraduates, prepares the candidates to take seriously the heavy workload they will receive as medical students and interns.

Second, while still students in medical school, they develop a sense of identification with those who are in the same situation and even learn to share the work with their peers so that it becomes more manageable. As Howard Becker and his associates (1961) point out, facing this common task with a sense of shared responsibility builds strong interpersonal loyalties among medical students. While the first two years of medical school generally consist of basic science courses, students spend their last year or two in clinical study, and some even take on medical responsibilities during this part of their training. Students who are given these responsibilities are most likely to see themselves as physicians even before receiving their degrees than those who do not have this kind of training.

Response to peers becomes even more important during internship and residency, when the trainees must learn to share caseloads and depend upon one another for information that they cannot assimilate from books or from the various medical experts with whom they come in contact. Interns and residents can be observed in hospital cafeterias spending their free time talking about medical procedures and the condition of patients. They read journals whenever possible, and very often this source of information is made available to interns and residents by unsolicited subscriptions heavily subsidized by the drug industry. Being knowledgeable about drugs is one way in which interns and residents keep the regard of their peers.

Peer control and evaluation occurs later in both a formal and an informal way. Licensing and certification examinations, minimal tests of competency, are administered by the medical profession to those who seek to practice in the various states. Board certification often permits licensed physicians to affiliate with a medical school, an important source of prestige in the medical profession, or to practice in certain other desirable settings. Informal peer control occurs when physicians assess whether a colleague has been Board-certified, keeps up with new treatment modalities, knows about the latest research, and receives referrals from prestigious members of the profession. In addition, services at other hospitals or academic departments may be evaluated according to whether the head of the same service or department at the medical school with which a physician is affiliated has good or bad things to say about the service or department in question. Old school ties are also very important in evaluating unknown medical facilities; that is, approval is more likely to take place when someone with whom a physician underwent training is identified as practicing at the facility.

The most humiliating penalty a unit director can impose upon a fellow physican is to to treat him not as a colleague but as one who needs day-by-day supervision in the way he practices medicine. This may be done privately or publicly. Obviously it is far more devastating to the physician's reputation when it is done in such a way that his peers are informed of his status. Supervision for an independent physician means he has lost the right to exercise his judgment and responsibility, the essential characteristics of a professional. It can be said that supervision is more degrading than a malpractice suit, since many fellow physicians will sympathize with a person who must face litigation when he was only trying to do his best as a doctor. Thus in many ways and at many stages in the career of the professional, informal mechanisms of social control are utilized to keep members of that field in line, ensuring solidarity within the community of equals.

This portrait of social control in the medical profession is not without problems for the professionals themselves and for the sociologist who is engaged in studying them. There is always potential conflict between collegial solidarity and the concern for competence. Choices will be made that are based on arbitrary and capricious standards. But this does not illustrate that social control is not at work, merely that it operates with less than complete efficiency.

In fact the law and the legitimate force behind it is only one form of social control. We are all under control, talking, behaving, failing to do or doing, at all times. Control is being exercised in an ordinary conversation to determine who may speak and when, sometimes to determine that one must speak, and always watching, though ever so subtly, each word that is uttered.

But ours is not a world of people on the lookout, fearful that their lives may be ruined by a malapropism, that they may be caught, if not with their pants down, at least with their shirt off, at an inappropriate time and place. The rules are so well known, so thoroughly ingrained, that they are followed with little awareness of that fact. This is evidence not of a lack of social control but of its overwhelming effectiveness.

GROUP BELONGING: THE REAFFIRMATION OF MEMBERSHIP

Human life has been characterized as group life. It is in groups that the social nature of human beings is refined and developed.

Primary socialization—the acquisition of knowledge, ability, and motivation—usually occurs within the confines of the group called "the family." But whether that first community is a nuclear family, a commune, a nursery, a tribe, or a combination of two or more of these, children learn to be part of some social entity and receive recognition for their contributions to it. Group membership provides the opportunity to be somebody and to establish solidarity with other people. We are all members, not of one group but of many; some we join voluntarily, and in others we are "signed up" without our knowledge and before we reach the age of consent.

One of the ways in which a person knows with certainty that he is accepted as a member is by being permitted to take part in activities in which the meaning of membership (and nonmembership as well) is made plain to all present. Social control takes place on most social occasions, but it is most evident to human beings when they are first permitted to exercise the rights of membership. Rites of passage remind everyone of their expected loyalties. Social control is not only a process to bring into line those members of a group who do not follow all the rules, who backslide, or who even willingly seek to leave the group and join other groups. It is primarily a way of keeping in line those who do not present overt indications that they are not living up to the expectations of others. The upright not only see what would happen if they consciously attempted to get out of line but also learn to appreciate the strength the group has in dealing with those who stray. As a result, belief in group norms may be increased through simple and even enjoyable activities, such as gossiping about others.

In this sense, social control may be conceived of as an informal interpersonal practice in groups which implicitly strengthens the bonds of social cohesion while it is overtly aimed at persons who may even be beyond the scope of the group's power to control. The process of social control has its greatest impact upon the persons actively engaged in doing it. It is largely a preventative activity rather than an effort to root out deviance. It is preventative insofar as it provides warnings to those who may sometimes waiver and brings those who follow the rules incumbent upon the members even closer together.

During the course of membership in most groups, there are times when people get together and engage in collective activities; they may catch up on what has gone on in one another's lives or comment on what other acquaintances or group members have or have not done. Reunions mark not only the passage of time but the importance of group life. On such occasions those who are not present may be discussed and their activities dissected and evaluated. The discussion of peers who are not present conveys certain things to the participants about their own relationship as well as about those who are the subjects of conversation. In engaging in such discussions, members extend to one another the right to hear not only what might be considered confidential information but also confidential opinions, an indication to another that he is trusted and considered part of some kind of inner circle. Gossiping about those who are absent on specific occasions may be considered to be a way in which members define the limits of tolerated and obligatory behavior. The first time one is privy to such activities serves as a ceremony of initiation as a full-fledged member of a group; it also serves as a warning.

As a means of social control, gossip keeps open the lines of communication to those not present. One of the cardinal rules of good gossiping is never to let the absent person know that you were gossiping about him. Such a rule indicates, again, that the intent of gossip is generally to affect those who hear it and are trusted, rather than the object of the tales. Most important, gossip usually does not attempt to isolate the person talked about but merely reminds the listener of the limits of approved behavior.

Other informal means of social control may be conceived of as being aimed more directly at the object of attention. Rumor operates in a way similar to gossip but is intended to stop deviant activities from continuing or becoming more organized and valued by the doer. (At least rumor works in this direction, even if this is not the intention of those responsible for it.) Rumor can become a "self-defeating" or a "self-fulfilling" prophecy. While it is intended to prevent matters from deteriorating or getting out of hand, it sometimes backfires, and people who were covertly engaged in isolated deviant activities may become defiant and seek to form alliances with others who are similarly situated. Heretics are usually more feared than sinners in churches and in informal groups as well. Defiance can be provoked by efforts at social control which are regarded as arbitrary, capricious, spiteful, or vindictive, and not aimed at correcting an injustice but simply aimed at destroying another person's reputation. In a legal sense, this kind of behavior can be considered equivalent to hearsay evidence, something that is unverified even though it may be verifiable, but that fails to be convincing because it does not emanate from a primary source.

While rumor can and often does aim at stopping suspected activity, sarcasm is directed toward the person who is present. Sarcasm is an acerbic form of humor that acts as a reprimand, reducing an issue to something unworthy of serious consideration. In this sense it cannot be responded to, for a response would only affect the standing of the object of the barb. In short, sarcasm stops a discussion or an action without allowing the recipient to make an issue out of what is happening to him. The object of these cutting remarks, when they are handled subtly, will appear foolish if he responds negatively.

Consider the following illustration. A group of women are playing cards, and one of them is singing while she and the others are trying to figure out their strategy. In order to get her to stop entertaining them and proceed with the game, the other women start commenting on her lovely voice. She has been noticed breaking a rule. The woman stops singing, and the others immediately stop commenting on her voice. Corrective efforts of this kind may be made on other occasions when a task at hand requires some concentration and involvement. Goffman (1961b) discusses how surgeons keep the attention of residents during a routine operation through the use of humor, irrelevant remarks, and similar devices. In general, sarcasm is used in a situation where everyone knows everyone else and each participant is expected to know what the rules are—stated or unstated. Each participant is believed to owe something to each of the other participants and to the purposes of the occasion. Getting people to respect one another occurs not only at ceremonial times, such as weddings and funerals, but in everyday life, when dignity and respect are equally important to those participating in group

activities. The person with the highest status in a group organized according to some ranking, as in a medical team, is expected to initiate efforts at social control that are preventive as
well as punitive.

Ridicule, in contrast to sarcasm, is generally aimed at the nonmember, the member-to-be, or the new member. As a form of
humor, it is crude and degrading, so that the object gets the point
easily. It requires a group in which the bond between members
is very strong but where each member is not always certain of his
own position in the hierarchy. This is why the most vocal objec-
tors to outsiders or new members are often the most deviant
members of a group, the people who have the most to prove, next
to the newcomers. Hazing in military academies, for example, is
generally done by the class most recently subject to the same
harassing treatment rather than by upperclassmen.

It is often the case that the content of ridicule could be used
against the user as well. Archie Bunker of television fame is
vulnerable to the same epithets and derisive expressions he applies to various ethnic groups. In fact, at least some members of
the audience for *All in the Family* probably laugh at the bigoted
Bunker because he is being ridiculed by the authors, although
there is unquestionably a part of the audience that identifies with
the bigotry (all of which is evidence that man is capable of inter-
preting what he hears and sees in the light of what he already
believes or wants to believe). It is easy for people who are upper
middle class and who carefully watch their language to lash out
at those whose mode of expression is less subtle. Working-class
figures like Archie can now be made fun of in front of a mass
audience because outspokenly bigoted behavior is no longer regarded as appropriate. Not too long ago, radio and stage comedi-
ans used dialect and even makeup in order to ridicule ethnic
groups. *Amos and Andy,* a radio program that had an audience as
large as that for *All in the Family,* put down black people, particularly those who used big words but only incorrectly, thus displaying ignorance and confirming the view of many Americans that
there is something ludicrous about blacks' being educated and
talking intelligently.

In American society, people who are pretentious, who put on
airs, who make claims to be better than everyone else, are subject
to the same kind of criticism today as in the 1930s. *The Beverly*

Hillbillies, a popular television program of the 1960s, used the incongruity of mountain folk living in opulent southern California to make that point. Television programming may give the social observer a better clue to popular morality than the study of public opinion or of sermons from the pulpit. What people laugh at and sympathize with can be considered a symbolic representation of underlying norms and practices which are difficult to talk about to an interviewer or a minister.

The Constraints of Group Membership

The form of a person's participation in a group's activities is strongly influenced by the almost continuous efforts of the group to keep people in line and reinforce the group's meaning to the membership. The return of members from a trip after they have been away for a time provides a strategic occasion for them to reaffirm their ties to one another and reemphasize the importance of the group. Herbert Gans (1962) reports that when some working-class people return to their group of neighbors, the major focus is on how good it feels to come back home rather than on how interesting it was to be in a foreign place. During a discussion of the events of the trip, they may dwell on incidents that point to the difficulties they encountered, how one might have been taken advantage of by strangers. Home territory and the protective aspects of group life are highlighted when people leave these physical and social environments.

Similar discussions take place in the home when a child has gone off to college or on an extended trip without the family. The parents will encourage the returning son or daughter to speak about how much he or she missed home cooking while away. The parents, in turn, will comment on how the child has changed since leaving home and the child will reassure the parents that he or she is really the same deep down inside. This kind of rupture in social relationships, even when it is encouraged and anticipated, has to be compensated for by an extensive set of verbal suggestions that matters are still the same between people despite long absences. Parents will continue to provide for their grown-up child away at school, by sending "care packages" of food and other homey reminders of the affiliations that still exist.

The recounting of adventures in travel and of the horrible conditions of life away from home is an opportunity to suggest just how important the group is to the member. Membership in peer groups may be far more important in a working-class community, which cannot, as a community, provide as much respect and recognition to the members in terms of occupational prestige and exclusiveness as is found in the middle class. Being a member of a peer group may be a way to be somebody when the large society, in the form of the boss, the professionals, the white-collar workers, does not extend that opportunity for recognition which all people need. The peer group for a working-class person is the society, which compensates for what the larger society refuses to pay in respect.

When people who are counted upon to give recognition and respect suddenly remove their supports or threaten not to provide them any longer to other members of a peer group, then the subject of social control may become the central focus of interaction between members. Gans (1962) notes that a member of a peer group who attempts to command another will be sanctioned for claiming to have greater authority, rank, and status than the other person. Since members are expected to uphold this concept of equality with each other, even when an outside conflict develops, such as a fight over damage to property, a member who attempts to be bossy will be regarded as breaking the rules.

In middle-class society, sanctions are invoked that attempt to shame a community member into holding up his end of respectability. This may occur, for example, if a person allows his property to become rundown or unkempt. Neighbors will offer to lend a lawnmower to someone on the block who has not mowed his lawn for some time. When this broad hint does not work, they may even go to the extreme of mowing the lawn for him. This overt act of contempt for the supposedly lazy neighbor does not begin to reveal the kind of private verbal abuse that must have led to such drastic action.

Ostracism and exclusion are perhaps the most severe penalties invoked against a person who is regarded as no longer following the rules and who no longer offers apologies or otherwise indicates that he is contrite. They are used when all else fails and when the rule violators are considered to be totally responsible for acts so outrageous that they should be made nonmembers of the group. These forms of social control operate on the surgical model of the spread of a disease, with contagion endangering the group and what it means to the members. Harold Garfinkel (1956) calls these occasions "degradation ceremonies." The seriousness of offense and punishment is often marked by high drama, and the outcast is handled in a ceremonious way, made to feel, along with the upright members of the group, the inevitability and irrevocability of the chain of events that led to his or her demise as a member.

The person subject to ostracism and exclusion may not even be around to receive the punishment because he may have been killed or may have fled from the group. In these circumstances, ostracism and exclusion still take place through efforts to explain the behavior of the person who committed the unspeakable act; the explanation serves to isolate him symbolically from the group. When a man climbed a tower on a Texas campus and killed and wounded some thirty people before being shot himself, the agents of social control were at a loss to offer an explanation of this act. An explanation was necessary, even though both perpetrator and victims were dead, in order to demonstrate that this is not the type of activity permitted to occur in society. Furthermore, the killer was white and American-born: white society could not even achieve cohesion by blaming the act on "one of them." The newspapers pointed out that the murderer had been convicted of gambling while a marine. But what redblooded American marine doesn't gamble? Along the same lines, the press discovered that he had once been convicted of poaching game in Texas. Again, is that so uncommon for a Texan to do? Finally, it was found that he had been under psychiatric care: Now the entire matter could be explained as the act of a demented man. "Building a case" is a task for those mandated to symbolically explain and condemn the person who took those lives. The task of repairing the social fabric when a meaningless and supposedly causeless event occurs involves restoring belief in the security of public places and trust in others. It is something that has to be done, even in the absence of the villain. As Emile

Durkheim has noted, punishment is designed to act upon the upright members of society even more than on the transgressors.

The end of public executions, such as hangings, may have increased the need for graphic reporting of punishments. While the public execution may never have prevented any would-be murderer from killing because of the possible punishment he might face—and one cannot be certain of this, but it is widely believed—it surely was an opportunity to see justice done and the restoration of the protection of members of society by the institutions designed to provide this protection. The basic and elemental ties of the member to the group remain firm only when there are occasions on which to reaffirm these ties. There are other occasions when people are kept apart rather than brought together. During such moments, when human needs may remain unmet, no new groups are formed to challenge the existing ways of doing things to accomplish the tasks at hand. The study of social control, then, also involves the study of the prevention of new alignments and affiliations, a subject that begins to touch on the interpersonal aspects of social change.

Social Control through Staying Apart: A Concept and a Case History

A great deal of social control in modern society takes the form of the maintenance of formality and coordination. Although one often thinks of norms as governing the respect one accords to the life and basic rights of others or how one carries out ukases of such significance that society might collapse (or so it appears) if they were violated, all-pervasive norms govern the small, unnoticed, reflexive, and tacitly understood modes of behavior in everyday life and in the most mundane instances. Much of this is a matter of controlling the intrusions of a person on others.

Modern society is characterized by a highly developed division of labor or differentiation of institutions. An outstanding example of this characterization is the common separation of home and workplace. People go to different places for different services. Decentralization means that people come into contact during the day with many people whom they do not know at all or with whom they share only limited interests. There are opportunities for conflict and cooperation beyond what those who occupy coordinative positions in organizations are capable of regulating. Peacekeeping in public places, for example, depends to a great extent on the self-constraint of those who come into contact with others. There are norms of keeping one's distance, which is another way of preventing the invasion of privacy or the development of uninvited intimacies.

In short, there are rules that make frequent contact between strangers possible. Norms concerning how to behave on a subway are not written down, but people learn how not to come into conflict with one another by avoiding provocation, providing appropriate respect for others in public by not staring or attempting to strike up conversations, and knowing how to be discouraging yet not impolite if someone else violates such norms. Movement on a street is like a choreographed dance, with people using their bodies, their facial expressions, their eyes to express their intentions, or what they would like others to think are their intentions. Since many public places are not demarcated as belonging to particular people or groups of people, those present indicate to others that they have a right to be present and that they ratify the right of others to be present as well.

Consider how people enter a public place such as a subway car or lunch counter. There is generally an effort on a person's part to disrupt ongoing activities as little as possible, even though there is no single focus and no event going on. One may take a seat where the most space exists, leaving some empty seats between oneself and the next person. When one is forced to squeeze in between two other people, the newcomer's facial expression and body will signify that he is aware of intruding, even if he has a perfect right to occupy that seat. One symbolically makes himself small and "squeezes" in, doing a kind of pantomime, even when adequate room is available on either side. Then the newcomer will glance slightly at the persons on his left and right before adjusting his eyes to look straight ahead. Interestingly, the person who fails to proffer deference to others and expresses, through either gestures or words, that he does not recognize their presence and their rights will himself be treated rudely. Others may stare at such a person, laugh, or even talk quite openly about how "some people have all the nerve."

In some kinds of situations involving service-giving organizations, it is more difficult to determine why people stay apart, particularly when they have common complaints about those organizations. Why is it that people who feel that things might be different, who can present cogent criticism of institutions, still do little about them? Why do people so frequently go along with organized ways of doing things rather than seek to change them? Suburban commuters whose trains are cancelled without explanation, for example, generally do very little but complain. They become resigned and cynical, and come to expect cancellations.

Other service organizations receive the same reluctant compliance when there is much to change. Sometimes organizations such as the courts or hospitals even offer a kind of freedom to engage in individualized pursuits while waiting to be served or to serve. This may be the way bureaucracies prevent the development of organized sources of resistance and change among clients.

It is often the case that being in the situation provides too little distance from these processes of social control to permit one to see them operate. Social psychologists who are concerned with the impact of physical space on human behavior, such as Robert Sommer, have noted that waiting rooms in airports have been deliberately arranged to reduce the possibility of people coming together and getting to know one another. Observers of psychiatric hospitals and institutions for mentally retarded people have indicated that when there is little room for privacy, dignity, and self-respect among residents, it is unlikely that the staff will extend it or that the residents will demand it. Those who direct these hospitals, institutions, and even airports defend their practices as being more efficient or less costly than efforts to promote greater opportunities for people to fraternize.

A sociological examination of how people present themselves may lead to an examination of the subtle and intriguing question of why people do not attempt to change things. Using our understanding of what happens when people are gathered and stacked within the confines of an organization in order to receive or give a service, we can consider the question of why something did *not* happen. Even when individual motivation to criticize the "system" is strong, often there is little criticism and seldom is there anything more concrete. Effective organizations may not only acquire standardized ways of dealing with clients and customers but also develop a capacity to manage the dissatisfactions of their clients and customers so as to prevent them from becoming a direct challenge to their practices.

People may become deeply engaged because various activities demand complete attention. Others may expect the performer of a particular role to give everything to it. Sometimes a task is not too difficult or involves little work, and various "side involvements," as Goffman calls them, are permitted. The student employee who inspects outgoing briefcases in the library is generally permitted to read while on duty, since the flow of traffic past his desk is not steady but irregular. A person who rides the subway may scan the other faces (although with real or feigned lack of curiosity or of any other intrusive sign), or he may read the advertisements, a newspaper, or a book. If one is traveling with a companion, conversation is permitted, and other passengers will object only if the noise level is extremely high. The major or main involvement of getting from one place to another does not require much concentration or effort if one is a passenger in a vehicle. In fact, overinvolvement in the role, as when a person is designated a "backseat driver," is regarded as inappropriate behavior. There is a great deal of room for people with time on their hands to get together with other people who are in the same situation. One of their common complaints concerns the slowness of service. They do little, however, to develop shared solutions to these problems of organization.

Many formal organizations or bureaucracies are deliberately conceived to achieve some goal or future state of affairs and find it desirable to prevent clients or lower-level personnel in the organization from getting more involved in their roles. The physical arrangements of waiting rooms and the activities of those who come into direct contact with the public are often expected to keep that public in line. Thus, clients in welfare offices or in outpatient medical-care settings often have to wait for long periods of time before receiving service. Those who give service to the government when called for jury duty are also asked to wait, sometimes for days on end.

Jury Duty: The Norm of Noninvolvement

The following case material, based on a field study conducted by one of the authors while serving on jury duty, reveals how people are kept apart despite common complaints and opportunities to develop definitions counter to those offered by the courts and their agents.

A detailed analysis of the experience of serving on juries suggests that the clerks of the court encourage disengagement from the main tasks with which jurors are normatively obliged to be concerned. This disengagement process is made viable by permissive treatment of prospective jurors through routines that even permit minor violations of the court's own rules. Jurors may return late from lunch without even receiving a mild rebuke.

This behavior of the clerks is in sharp contrast to the treatment of citizens when they are first screened and separated into groupings headed for civil or criminal proceedings. The courtesies shown by clerks once these procedures are completed suggest that a form of social control is utilized to permit them to handle a persistent and difficult problem: how to keep persons in a state of readiness—that is, available for service—despite the fact that jurors have no control over the major function of the court—namely, the trial of arraigned defendants. Furthermore, the formal sanctions of the courts (fines or even prison for failure to serve on the jury) are enforceable but are quite remote from the lives of those called. In fact, they are ineffective from the point of view of the goals of the court.

Because of their own uncertainty about the scheduling of trials, the clerks ask prospective jurors to set aside their main reason for being there and merely stay on the premises, using their time as they please. Getting the prospective juror to regard himself as being out of that role is an important factor in mitigating discontent with the entire procedure. To some extent, officials can determine group formation by encouraging those who might become leaders by virtue of their occupational status to continue these roles on the premises. Those who can bring work with them (for example, free professionals) will be more satisfied than those who cannot.

The initiation of the jury trial is totally in the hands of the judge and the two adversaries. The clerk must stand and wait for his call, much in the manner of the prospective juror. How, then, does the clerk manage to create predictability where there is none? How does this constructed predictability preclude the strong possibility of the formation of a group with contrasting expectations?

Although uncertain about when trials will begin, the clerks do possess some information about the workings of the court. In addition, they can estimate whether any prospective juror will be likely to serve the minimum or maximum number of days. The clerks in the jury waiting room also give the prospective juror his first sense of what is going on.

A person who is scheduled to serve as a juror has his first contact with the court system at a building in which long lines of prospective jurors present themselves and their admission slips to two clerks. These clerks process people brusquely: they are obliged to move about 750 people within a one-hour period into a large and inhospitable room with benches. They explain nothing to the prospective jurors. The same questions are asked of each person, which to the novice appear to be largely arbitrary: for example, "Are you a New York City employee?" After about a half hour of waiting a clerk appears and reads off a long list of names, telling people to go to another room on the same floor if their names are called. This process of selection is handled quickly and is designed, again, to move large numbers of people about with great speed. For those who cannot follow the directives of the clerk with alacrity, a degrading remark is thrown in to speed the delinquent on his way: "Speak up, John. Ah, raise your hand higher. You weren't listening to me."

After this herding, selection, and reherding process members of the panel are sent to a jury waiting room. In contrast to the brusqueness of the initial encounter, the clerk in charge here has a benign manner. He is not rushed and begins to provide meaningful information. At this time the individual is first able to develop some sense of what is going on and what is expected of him. This clerk performs his task with some humor and gives the impression of being an understanding man. He explains that this is the end of a session and a time when the judges rotate from criminal to civil court, and vice versa. Since the judges are about to leave, they are hesitant about beginning new cases that might interfere with the rotation process. They are currently engaged in "cleaning up" their calendars. The clerk anticipates that most prospective jurors will be released after serving the minimum five days.

Although the clerk makes no promises, he does provide useful information that allows the prospective juror to weigh his chances of serving the shortest possible legally required term. Furthermore, he gives little reason for complaint about the hours of service. People are required to be present from ten A.M. to four P.M., with one hour off for lunch and are told that they will be released early if the judge decides that a jury will not be selected that day.

The clerk in the jury waiting room also encourages the prospective juror to step outside this role for most of the time he will serve. Phones, toilets, and a smoking room are available. Individuals may go downstairs to the lobby for candy, food, and tobacco so long as they sign a sheet of paper at the front of the room on leaving and returning. Conversation is permitted, and magazines and writing paper are provided. A few tables are located in the smoking room, and people who wish to work or play cards are encouraged to do so. (No gambling is permitted, however.) Thus lower-level court officials encourage everyone to exhibit distance from tasks. Everyday routines can be carried on within the confines of the setting.

For the most part, those who are able to bring work with them are most suited to continue their outside roles. In addition, status distinctions according to extrinsic signs, such as dress, speech, type of newspapers and books read, are used as the basis for establishing acquaintanceships. It should be noted, however, that those who are the most likely to become opinion leaders in this setting are also those most likely to be able to perpetuate their vocational roles. Many of the teachers present, for example, are busy marking examination papers. By keeping to their conventional occupational roles, these potential opinion leaders are able to discourage others from engaging them in conversation. Furthermore, those who do converse are generally in pairs rather than in larger groupings. The only cliques that form are according to the most general and overt signs of status, such as among some ethnically similar people and the few women who volunteer to serve on a jury.* That clique formation is precluded by the freedom to be disengaged in this setting is affirmed by the fact that many people who brought newspapers with them during the first two days brought books on the third day. Conversation was also less frequent by this time. The prospective jurors had settled down to an uneventful stay, consisting merely of "serving time."

In many respects, one could conduct oneself outside the role of prospective juror. Many people spent several hours outside the jury waiting room without receiving even a mild rebuke from the clerk. Furthermore, many people arrived long after ten in the morning or returned late from lunch without sanction. The heaviest sanctions were invoked upon those who failed to appear after the first day: they were later recalled to serve yet another term. This penalty was known to all in the waiting room, and few persons provoked it.

The jury waiting room was hardly conducive to informal social organization. Essentially it was an auditorium with fixed rows of seats. Direct face-to-face interaction was difficult to achieve. The closeness of the seats to each other made individuals refrain, when given the option, from sitting side by side with others. Leaving a seat in between as a sign of respect to the other's personal integrity meant that few openings were provided for engaging in conversation.

Some circles were formed in the smoking room. However, the population there, with the exception of those who worked at the tables, was basically transient. It was not a comfortable room in which to remain for a long period of time; it was not air-conditioned, and the traffic was heavy. The telephones were located in this room, and those who sought conversation were often interrupted by a "phoner" wishing to change money. In addition, voices were modulated in deference to those who were working, and their presence at the tables made card-playing awkward. People began to treat the hot, busy smoking room as a place

*Since the time of this experience, women have become equal to men in their obligations to serve on juries.

where it was inappropriate to linger unless one was engaged in paperwork.

The conditions for maintaining side concerns or concerns with outside roles were so good that one seldom heard a complaint about not "being used." In many ways, the prospective jurors were lulled into a false sense of security. The feeling was that the worst thing that could happen would be a requirement to sit there for six days instead of the minimal five. This view was reinforced during the witnessing of "graduating exercises" for the previous week's selectees, who now became known as second-week jurors. They had served their time, but none of them had been empaneled. At this point, there was an air of confidence that service on a jury had become unlikely.

The actual process of being empaneled destroyed the taken-for-granted notions of this predictable system. Many people complained aloud, but to no one in particular, that it wasn't fair to empanel them so late in the term of service. Although many would have welcomed the opportunity to serve on a jury earlier, most were not so eager now that they had become second-week jurors and anticipated imminent release. The likelihood that they would soon be sitting in judgment over another human being also shocked many who had never served before. They had not been prepared for active service; main involvements had suddenly become reactivated, and yet a sense of justice was threatened by the prospect of actual jury duty. They had been led to believe that they could serve according to the letter of the law, but not the spirit of the law.

An event of this type is but an example of what occurs in all aspects of life and on many occasions. The norms of society had governed the manner in which people were thrown together although they were strangers and had a limited time-span during which they might be co-present. The gathering of these persons was constructed in such a manner that its purpose, for most participants, would be thwarted, and norms made possible the reduction of frustration. Togetherness, however, could not become intimacy in this setting any more than on a bus or subway; both the physical setting and the manner of handling interpersonal contact worked to achieve the normatively expected distance.

While it is more convincing to discuss how people are obliged to get together to achieve their objectives, it is sometimes useful, as in this preceding case study, to examine how people are kept apart and thus in line. By encouraging what Goffman (1961a) calls "colonization"—the process of making oneself comfortable in an involuntary situation—prospective jurors were able to "flesh out their lives" and make constructive use of leisure time for their own personal ends or amusement. At the same time, the courts and their methods of collecting potential jurors remain unchanged.

The analysis of the jury waiting room also demonstrates that possibilities for deviant behavior and even of the organization of efforts for social change are present in all situations. If all situations are alterable, it still requires an effort to make the alterations through directed activity. Society is a human product subject to natural limitations, but there is a tendency to regard social arrangements as having a fixed character. Even when norms are challenged or are found to be unworkable, there is a strong tendency to believe that they are right and proper.

Norms represent the security and social recognition of individuals. Why people involuntarily conform (and why they do not) is a complex question, involving the dynamics of membership in groups. As a member, even a marginal member, a person may receive social recognition and security. The behavior of upright members of society may be foolish from the point of view of the deviant, but that behavior may become utterly predictable to him. The relationship between conformity and deviance is the major content of the study of norms and human behavior, the very stuff out of which social life is made.

4

Explaining Behavior

Although every society does its utmost to gain the greatest possible obedience to its major rules, and to the minor ones as well, violations occur, and sometimes they fall outside the limits of what the society can tolerate with impunity. Whether man is by nature a cooperative animal and is turned into a hedonistic, pleasure-demanding, and often violent one by society or whether the opposite model of man is more congruent with reality is a matter that philosophers and psychologists as well as sociologists will long ponder. But social groups do have their rules, measures are taken to induce people to follow them, and sanctions are available for use against those who do not.

It is sometimes said that all people, even the most rebellious and anti-authoritarian, are norm-followers. The burglar, it is pointed out, follows the same eating habits as other members of the society, walks, talks, and gestures as his compatriots do, drives on the right side of the street, stands at the accepted distance from another while talking to him, covers his mouth while yawning, shows his unhappiness at funerals—and one could continue. This does not, of course, demonstrate that he is

76

a good, essentially law-abiding, and conforming member of society in all respects save one, for we cannot count his conforming acts and contrast the total with the number of his nonconforming or deviant acts. It does mean, however, that the norms of society are most pervasive, that one is unlikely to be able to interact with others without following most of the norms, and that they guide people through the entire day.

People generally conform to the rules of their groups for many reasons. For one thing, it has been inculcated in them, sometimes from earliest childhood, that these are the right and proper ways and that any other way would be unthinkable. They not only have been educated and socialized into these rules but have come to accept them fully, unthinkingly, on faith, without reservations. When the rules involve the everyday facets of human behavior, Alfred Schutz (1964) referred to them as the taken-for-granted aspects of human conduct. With this phrase he suggested that these are the ways people perform most acts of their life, without stopping to question whether they are morally right, proper, easy, comfortable; this is just how things are done.

Accordingly, we anticipate that other people will behave in ways which will allow us to regard them with approval. It is taken for granted among cohabiting couples that one may enter a bedroom without knocking. Friends often borrow books and other small items from each other without asking, but when it comes to money or an apartment or a car we expect that the would-be borrower will first get our approval. Harold Garfinkel (1967) has designed experiments in which the taken-for-grantedness of situations is deliberately violated in order to see whether these rules concerning familiar social relationships exist. While the ethics of these experiments has been subject to criticism by other social scientists, notably Kai Erikson (1967), they are persuasive in validating the concept that much of everyday social life is integrated by people's willingness to take the motives of others for granted.

Even when people violate the rules, we expect that they will do so with a great deal of propriety. While people may enter into adulterous relationships, we do not expect that a man or a woman will bring both spouse and lover to the same party. People today may cohabit openly but often find it awkward to disclose this fact to others because the terms available to designate common-law mates have not received full validation. Students may use the folksy expressions "my old man" or "my old lady," but older people cannot apply such terms to their relationships. Lately, the term "consort" has been suggested as appropriate and more dignified than the informal argot of the campus.

People conform to the rules not only because they have learned them so well and believe in them so strongly but also because there is often no road open to them except conformity. The physical and cultural world is built around these rules. One enters a restaurant and there are seats at a counter or at a table, and there are either waiters or a self-service system in operation, or both. Wherever one sits and whatever may be the method of service, the eating place is constructed in such a manner as to make that method of obtaining food possible. If there is no self-service, there will be no counter to which one can go and select food, no trays waiting to bring it back to a table, only a door leading to a kitchen which, it is indicated explicitly or implicitly, the customer is not to enter. You cannot sit on the floor in a corner, as you might in a student lounge or in a foreign land, place your dishes on the floor, and eat from that position: there are no corners available for that purpose; the floor is probably uninviting; people would stare at you as if you were crazy; and that that is not the way things are done is part of your taken-for-granted world.

The reasons people conform are many. Among them are the specific rewards or positive sanctions awaiting those who do things in the manner that they are supposed to be done. These are rewards in the form of affection, acceptance by family, peers, and others, monetary rewards, sexual rewards, pleasure rewards, whatever the case may be.

The causes of conformity and of rule violation are infinite in the sense that there is an individual situation that confronts one person who makes a decision. But social science is interested in the origin of deviance in a broader context. That is, do people violate rules because of innate biological urges (such as aggression or compulsivity) that are incompatible with social living, or are there primarily psychological reasons that derive from the individual's temperament, personal background, and idiosyncratic experiences? Or can the reasons for rule violation be located in the nature of the social structure?

The major focus of sociological interest is explaining not the behavior of one person but of groups, or the frequency of such behavior and the fluctuations among many subgroups of a society or from one time and place to another. It is important to know why one individual commits suicide or becomes alcoholic or abandons wife and child. Sociology, however, is more concerned with the incidence of such activities, how the numbers of persons involved vary with social class, race, age, or social system.

The major social explanations for the prevalence of disvalued behavior are anomie theory, learning theories (particularly differential association), conflict theory, and social disorganization and heterogeneity. In addition, there is the matter of societal reaction (or labeling), which does not seek to explain the deviance itself but rather tries to account for the consequences that result from the negative attitudes toward it. Societal reaction will therefore be handled in a separate section of this book; other major perspectives are summarized in the following pages.

Anomie

Literally and etymologically, anomie is a state of normlessness. A truly normless society is a contradiction in terms—a social, not merely a political, condition of anarchy, thus probably precluding the existence of human society. "Anomie" can be used to describe what has been called "relative normlessness," which itself is an ambiguous term: It can mean, on the one hand, that there are many areas of life not governed by norms, or that the norms are relatively weak in the hold they have on many people. "Anomie" may be used as indicating "too many norms," which lose their hold because people do not know where to turn in conflicting loyalties. As a concept, anomie gained prominence in sociology when it was used by Emile Durkheim in the late 1890s to describe a state in which the bonds holding individuals to the society were extremely weak. According to Durkheim, this could account for some instances of suicide.

In a landmark essay on deviant behavior and anomie, Robert Merton (1938) utilized Durkheim's basic concept of social cohesion and alienation but went on to suggest that in some societies there is a deep schism between the goals with which the people are inculcated, goals that they must attain if they are to be successful and fulfilled members of that group, and the acceptable or institutionalized means for attaining these goals. In small, primitive, traditionalist, or highly religious societies, this dichotomy is less likely to exist; it thrives in modern, industrialized, impersonal, and secular societies, especially in the United States as a result of the development of the Protestant work ethic and the striving for money and other signs of financial success. In the United States, one has to "make it" in the world—this is emphasized and doubly emphasized— and he who fails to make it is a general failure. On the other hand, probably because of the decline of supernatural religion and the rise of secularism, American society teaches the norms for achieving these ends but fails to inculcate the significance of abiding by normative means and does not offer large numbers of people access to these institutionally endorsed methods of reaching success goals. Anomie is the state of conflict that develops between the goals one has internalized and the means one improvises or employs when the accepted methods of reaching such goals are largely blocked. Anomie, for Merton, is "a breakdown in the cultural structure, occurring particularly when there is an acute disjunction between the cultural norms and goals and the socially structured capacities of members of the group to act in accord with them."

In Merton's view of the world, social control has not failed; deviance, one might say, is not so much an indicator of the failure of social control as a sign of its success. Man is not a bundle of impulses seeking immediate gratification but controlled by or imprisoned in society. "The image of man as an untamed bundle of impulses," he writes, "begins to look more like a caricature than a portrait." Merton, rejecting this, sought "to discover how some *social structures exert a definite pressure upon certain persons in the society to engage in nonconforming rather than conforming conduct*" (italics in original).

The pressure against conformity derives from a conflict between the ends set forth as goals that all should seek to attain and the means available for reaching these goals. When people are unable to arrive at the goals by the socially accepted means, they have a number of possible choices open to them. These Merton arranged in what has come to be the most famous paradigm in sociology:

Merton's Paradigm: Anomie and the Ends-Means Conflict

	Ends	Means
Conformity	+	+
Innovation	+	−
Ritualism	−	+
Retreatism	−	−
Rebellion	±	±

Why should there be a conflict between ends and means in many modern societies, and particularly in the United States? The country's open class system not only motivates people to struggle for monetary success goals but also entices them into that struggle with promises that they can achieve the ends. "In this setting," according to Merton, "a cardinal American virtue, 'ambition,' promotes a cardinal American vice, 'deviant behavior.'"

Merton (1957:146) sees considerable value consensus even in a conflict-ridden and pluralistic society:

> It is only when a system of cultural values extols, virtually above all else, certain *common* success-goals *for the population at large,* while the social structure rigorously restricts or completely closes access to approved modes of reaching these goals *for a considerable part of the same population,* that deviant behavior ensues on a large scale. [Italics in original.]

In defense of the concept that Americans are overwhelmingly involved in the success rat-race, Merton (1957:136–37) writes:

> To say that the goal of monetary success is entrenched in American culture is only to say that Americans are bombarded on every side by precepts which affirm the right or, often, the duty of retaining the goal even in the face of repeated frustration. Prestigeful representatives of the society reinforce the cultural emphasis. The

family, the school, and the workplace—the major agencies shaping the personality structure and goal formation of Americans—join to provide the intensive disciplining required if an individual is to retain a goal that remains elusively beyond reach, if he is to be motivated by the promise of a gratification which is not redeemed.

It can be argued that Merton seems to be overlooking the peer group as a major force "shaping the personality structure and goal formation of Americans." However, taking this force into account makes his case stronger, not weaker. Even those who consider themselves counterculturalists have used the life-styles to their advantage by being successful songwriters, entertainers, and "hip capitalists" who live off the youth culture. In using athletics as an example, Merton might have made his case stronger had he contrasted the goal of winning with the use of acceptable means (or, one might say, the alternative goal) of playing for fun, sport, camaraderie, and entertainment of oneself and others, without regard to the score or the coveted victory. As a matter of fact, winning in sports contests seems to have become for many athletes and coaches a means, not an end: the means to financial rewards and commercialized glory. In any case, the gratification is in the end result, not in the participation. The goal of winning the game, rather than "winning under the rules of the game," is perhaps nowhere so apparent as in the sports arena.

As a concept of deviance, a theory explaining the forms it takes, anomie is not entirely successful and, in fact, leaves a great deal to be subjected to further study, elucidation, and validation. As Merton points out, it may be too ambitious to attempt to bring forth a single theory of deviance to explain all instances, all people, all types of behavior; it may be necessary, at least at this stage of human knowledge, to have middle-range theories that will explain a smaller portion of the deviant behavior. And as such, Merton's major thesis would be that lack of access to strongly inculcated goals produces deviance in a society in which there is little emphasis on the need to adhere to ethical and proper activities in life patterns. The major instance of deviance would involve monetary success goals, which are certainly blocked off to many persons; the reason people forge checks, swindle, commit acts of bribery, rob, embezzle, blow up safes, steal, burglarize, is not that they need money (this they do, and have since money was first used) but that American culture teaches them that they have to live high, to have and always accumulate more, but it does not offer masses of people opportunities to obtain the unlimited amounts they desire except through these immoral and illegal methods. People find different (Merton would say "new") ways of getting what they have been taught to want, envy, and admire in others; the result is crime for monetary gain. Crime may also, of course, be motivated by success goals other than financial gain. Thus we have Watergate, for which anomie theory offers almost a perfect key to an understanding of the motivation of the principal participants.

Learning Theory

For decades, if not centuries, students of human behavior have argued the question of whether nature or nurture is the greater influence. Among those thinkers who have favored environment as an explanation of how people behave, Edwin Sutherland, for many years the towering personality in American criminology, focused on how people learn to act in certain specific ways and how their modes of activity are transmitted through various cultural agencies, particularly to youth. Theories of this type flowered under the influence of Sutherland, who developed what came to be known as "differential association," but in various ways they can all be traced back to nineteenth-century sociology and criminology. Although the earlier adherents of such views have often been criticized and their major theses well-nigh discarded, it is possible that some of their ideas can be synthesized with those of the later cultural transmissionists and that the result can explain much in modern-day deviant behavior.

Essentially, the cultural transmissionists took sides on the great debate regarding heredity and environment and, furthermore, in answering the question of whether one must look to deviant people, to determine what was different or "wrong" about them, or to the society, to see what it contributed to making antisocial behavior "necessary" or possible, they synthesized the two. The deviant was indeed different from others, not only in how he behaved, but also in his mental-psychological attitudes; and this difference was nurtured in a social milieu that might be called "criminogenic."

Late in the nineteenth century, Gabriel Tarde (1843–1904) developed what he termed a theory of imitation. He saw criminal behavior as very much like normative behavior in the sense that there was little innovative about it and seldom a new form that was other than a slight adaptation of the old. Criminals, like everyone else, Tarde contended, imitated the ways of people they had met, heard about, or known of in one way or another. But they imitated other criminals, not law-abiding or "good" people.

According to Tarde (1912 ed.:278), if one studies the memoirs of police or local magistrates, one perceives

> by means of the similarity of the process employed by malefactors of the same region and of the same period, by means of the local color and the historical color which distinguishes the criminal fauna adapted to each locality and to each time, the preponderance of the "social factors" in the production of the offense and the delinquent. The criminal always imitates somebody, even when he originates; that is to say, when he uses in combination imitations obtained from various sources. He always needs to be encouraged by the example and approval of a group of men, whether it be a group of ancestors or a group of comrades, whence arises the duality of the crime because of custom and the crime because of fashion. It is precisely in this respect that the criminal is a social being, and that as such he is responsible.

When Sutherland developed a learning theory of criminal and deviant behavior, he appeared on the surface to depart from any theory of imitation. Fundamentally, Sutherland did not reject Tarde's outlook so much as modify it, primarily in his contention that behavior was learned, not by imitation, but by association with those who had already learned and nurtured it. In other words, Sutherland claimed, it was taught, whereas this element is essentially absent from the imitation theories.

Criminal behavior is learned, and it is learned in interaction with other persons, with intimate personal groups already committed to such types of conduct. One learns from them the values, attitudes, and drives, but particularly whether the laws or other rules of behavior are defined in a favorable or unfavorable manner. The violator is one whose associations have been mainly with people having an excess of unfavorable definitions toward the rules of society. He not only learns contempt for rules of conduct but also learns how to violate these norms (and even that certain forms of violation are available for those inclined in such direction).

If all behavior, normative as well as deviant, is learned, then the reason some people grow up to pursue the nonnormative path is that they have had more meaningful associations with those already engaged in the deviant way than with people who conform. The criminal is not inventive, and he imitates (in Sutherland's view) not because he has been exposed to mass media and propaganda, but because he has learned the "wrong way" from others already enmeshed in the criminal life.

The important point in this approach is not that certain social or economic conditions found in a given area give rise to a large amount of antisocial behavior, but that the large amount of antisocial behavior in a given area turns out to be self-perpetuating. People pass this down through role models, peer-group pressure, parental and fraternal influence, and sometimes actual instruction.

Sutherland's theory does not deny that slums breed delinquency and specifies how: he claimed that there is a social environment in the slums that fosters and sustains criminal behavior. For the same reason, so-called correctional homes for youth, reform schools, and juvenile prisons, under whatever name they existed, were breeding grounds for crime, because there the youth was given the opportunity to associate almost exclusively with those already involved and, moreover, with those who could teach him the techniques for the commission of the act.

Although it is true that some forms of deviant behavior require a good deal of skill in order to perform the act and not be apprehended, or even in order to enjoy the experience, this is not true of other forms. But even those acts requiring skill are often learned alone, by trial and error. Pickpocketing, lock-picking, safe-blowing, and bad-check writing are among those deviant behaviors that require lessons, and, in rare instances, things akin to classes and schools have been known to exist for this purpose.

Certainly, spies are sent to school and trained in a systematic manner to commit kidnapping, murder, and arson. But the techniques of many criminal acts are never learned. (Perhaps those who never learn are the people who get caught most easily; they botch their jobs, one might say.) This is true of assaults, rapes, murders of passion, and probably purse snatching and other street robberies. Furthermore, and this seems to be a major criticism of differential-association theory, some deviant acts are committed because one has learned the techniques *in association* with the most upright and conforming teachers. This can be said of embezzlement, tax fraud, and other white-collar crimes: One can pick up several of the techniques and a good deal of the necessary information while taking a course in accountancy or even bookkeeping. Techniques for committing crimes are learned by policemen and detectives, by students of criminology and deviant behavior, from the most well-meaning teachers and writers. Some of these police and students use the information and opportunities for criminal purposes.

Although the simple assumption with which this theory starts —namely, that criminal behavior is learned—would seem to many to be self-evident, Sheldon Glueck (1956) denies it in a powerful critique of differential association. Glueck writes:

> What is there to be learned about simple lying, taking things that belong to another, fighting and sex play? Do children have to be taught such natural acts? If one takes account of the psychiatric and criminological evidence that involves research into the early childhood manifestations of antisocial behavior, one must conclude that it is not delinquent behavior that is learned: that comes naturally. It is rather *non*delinquent behavior that is learned. Unsocialized, untamed, and uninstructed, the child resorts to lying, slyness, subterfuge, anger, hatred, theft, aggression, attack, and other forms of asocial behavior in its early attempts of self-expression and ego formation. [Italics in original.]

As many critics have pointed out, one must determine why it is that criminal lawyers, who have most of their associations with criminals, do not themselves become criminals. (At least, it is comforting to assume that this is true of the majority of them.)

How can one account for the "one bad kid in the family" syndrome—the situation in which several brothers and sisters are brought up in one home, subjected to essentially the same parental associations and values, mingle in the same neighborhood with a similar group of friends, go to the same schools; yet one brother drifts into a life of crime as the others become schoolteachers, doctors, lawyers, clergymen, or mechanics? How does one account for the large number of people who associate with gangs during their adolescence and yet mature into law-abiding respectable citizens? Did they start with different biological-temperamental makeups, or were they subject to the influences of seemingly small events that changed their life patterns? Can one conclude that truth demands a combination of both?

Finally, Sutherland saw the teaching of criminality entirely in terms of face-to-face association. Actually, the evidence would indicate that one learns to want to be criminal, to know about criminals and to have criminal interests and desires, from contact with ideas as much as with people, and sometimes from contact with people who are not at all criminally inclined themselves. As for the process of learning how to commit an act, it is not always learned from others who already have the skill.

Developing his theory before the television era, Sutherland underestimated the effect of the mass media upon learning. In a period when there is almost universal literacy in the Western world, when television, radio, and newspapers are reaching millions with a single message at all times, one can no longer discount the media as a major criminogenic force. Television never tells anyone to do anything "wrong," but it depicts wrong, suggests it, makes known that it is taking place, shows how it is done, and offers it as an alternative to anyone watching and listening. Then it gives the arguments against that alternative, but the arguments may be far from persuasive to people who are vulnerable to suggestion.

The language of Sutherland's original theory, and of the controversy that has been waged over it, centers upon crime and delinquency, not upon deviance in a more general sense. Yet the theory may be more tenable if it is extended. It is weakened, not strengthened, by the inclusion of references to lawbreaking and attitudes toward the law. People do not learn respect or disrespect for the law so much as they internalize certain behaviors as being the appropriate ones for themselves, and others as being inappropriate. To the extent that there is conformity, normative behavior, and law-abidingness, it is more a matter of the relative enticements of "right" and "wrong," the fear of punishment, and the strength of the teaching-and-learning process. "In our American society," Sutherland's original statement reads, "these definitions [of the legal codes as favorable or unfavorable] are almost always mixed." If this is so, and it appears to be, then it is not ignorance or disapproval of the law that is here being learned but a perspective toward propriety, tradition, authority, the official culture.

In the end, the theory of differential association leaves much unanswered. It does not tell us why there is widespread deviance, delinquency, or criminality in a given area or ethnic group, but it does suggest why this type of behavior persists. It does so because seeds are already planted, and newcomers entering a neighborhood, children growing into adolescence, become exposed to those who are already there and already committed to crime. This will tell us why cops entering the police force with high ideals become easily corrupted, as Arthur Niederhoffer (1967) so forcefully demonstrated, and why sometimes immigrants from abroad have a higher delinquency rate than they had in the area from which they came. But such a theory cannot cope with the basic cause of high or low crime and deviance rates, which will vary from place to place and from time to time. It does not tell us, for example, why suburban, middle-class, or upper-class deviance comes about at certain times, then flowers or declines.

In conclusion, compared to other approaches, differential-association theory is better equipped to explain the extent to which deviance results from social organization and is based on the same processes of socialization and social control that make for conformity. Its foremost contribution is the proposition that deviance is learned, not inborn or inherited. People sometimes tend to forget this and to avoid asking whether it is also learned from the major role models of the society—from celebrities, top politicians, and other important figures who teach corruption, cynicism, and racism to the population. Some members of the society interpret and act on this lesson in the only way open to them: by committing white-collar crime, predatory crime, fraud, and the like. However, differential-association theory often overlooks this relationship between patterned evasion of the rules and the points of contact with the larger society. In other theories, particularly those revolving around conflict in a heterogeneous society, these points of contact are regarded as crucial to understanding the norms, those who comply with them, and those who violate them.

Culture Conflict and Heterogeneity

The idea of organized conflict as an explanation for deviance has been popular for more than a century, but, treated by various schools of thought, it has taken on many different forms. It can be traced to Marxism, particularly to the philosophy of Hegel, from which Karl Marx derived the concept of the dialectic—the clash of antithetical forces—as a mechanism for social change. Marx applied this concept primarily to class conflict within a society; the Marxists used it to explain why some groups in power could commit predatory acts, steal, and plunder and yet avoid being labeled criminals, while others were driven by the struggle for survival to commit acts that they knew were subject to punishment in the society.

Marxism and Conflict Theory

In the half-century preceding the Russian revolution, numerous European scholars specializing in crime and deviance turned to Marxism for an all-encompassing explanation. The Marxist perspective not only explained the existence of crime but also offered a clear prescription for its diminution and eventual disappearance. Rejecting the Freudian view of man as basically an impulse-driven animal seeking immediate gratification and held in check only by external forces that imposed a moral order or threatened punitive retaliation, Marxism offered an image of humanity corrupted by a socioeconomic system of class conflict and exploitation.

Foremost among European thinkers who focused on the economic nature of many crimes, particularly in the period between World Wars I and II, was William A. Bonger (1932), a Dutch criminologist and sociologist. Numerous deviant acts grew out of economic need, he said, and they were conceptualized as crime only by a ruling class that was itself engaged in plunder. These lower-class or proletarian transgressions were obviously the result of capitalist exploitation. But capitalism could also be used to account for the acts of the greedy (later called white-collar crime) as arising from the competitive spirit and the drive for profit. As for other forms of deviance—alcoholism, acts of senseless and uncontrolled passion, sexual immorality, and the like—they were seen by socialists as signs of the degeneration of moral values in a capitalist society that thrived on institutionalized inequality, racism, and sexism.

With the success of the Russian revolution, many enthusiasts entertained utopian dreams: They expected society to gradually renounce deviance as it moved toward socialist goals. The continued existence of deviance was for a time explained by the socialization and education of many citizens under the old tsarist regime in Russia. As a new generation, born after the revolution, grew to maturity, it was believed by some that they would be nurtured on the ideals of the days of October and would not be motivated to perform antisocial acts. By the mid-1970s, the majority of Soviet residents were those born and reared after the revolution, so that the argument about the residual effects of tsarist teachings was seldom heard.

There is no consensus on the characterization of the Soviet state. Does it embody Marxist principles, or is it a betrayal of them? Should one look to China rather than to the Soviet Union for an indication of how the problem of deviance is resolved in a communist country? How successful has the Soviet Union been in reducing deviance and at what costs, as well as with what benefits, to the Russian people? An answer to such questions is hard to get. Statistics on deviance in the Soviet Union and China are for the most part unavailable. Nonetheless, it appears that alcoholism is a major problem in Russia, perhaps as much as ever; that sexual deviance, including prostitution and homosexuality, is less common than in the Western world; and that robbery, including even crime rings, though less organized and not so powerful as their counterparts in America, is not rare.

This would appear to cast doubt on the validity of Marxist explanations of deviance, although many socialists do not consider either the Soviet Union or China to be, at this stage in their development, exemplars of Marxist-organized societies.

The Marxist analysis of all aspects of social relations revolves around the central themes of exploitation, alienation, class consciousness, class conflict, and oppression. Wrongful acts are thus defined by a small group of persons who own the means of production, are wealthy, have political and military power, and control educational and other institutions. The state serves as the executive committee of the bourgeoisie, not mediating class and other conflicts but generating them and utilizing them in the interests of the ruling group. The preservation of the state and broad acceptance of loyalty to it are predicated on maintenance of the illusion that it represents all the people and protects everyone's interests equally. Its role as a force for stability in the constant struggle among hostile classes and its contribution to the institutionalization and channeling of conflict into legally prescribed means must be constantly obscured in order to hide its true nature as a political combatant allied with the owners and managers of capital.

For adherents of this view, widespread deviance is an expression of conflict among hostile groups and as such is a form of social protest. In the low level of consciousness of class interests, the deviant is often deflected in his struggle for survival and turns his weapons against members of his own class.

Marx (1963 ed.) further emphasized the place of crime in capitalist society and its integration into the economy:

> A philosopher produces ideas, a poet poems, a clergyman sermons, a professor compendia, and so on. A criminal produces crime. . . . The criminal produces not only crimes but also criminal law. . . . the whole of the police and of criminal justice, constables, judges, hangmen, juries, etc. While crime takes a part of the super-

fluous population off the labor market and thus reduces competition among the laborers—up to a certain point preventing wages from falling below the minimum—the struggle against crime absorbs another part of this population. Thus, the criminal comes in as one of those natural "counterweights" which bring about a correct balance and open up a whole perspective of "useful" occupations.

Marxist historians—for example, E. P. Thompson (1964), George Rudé (1969), and E. J. Hobsbawm (1963)—have pointed out that crime may be regarded as a prepolitical expression of social-class formation. Banditry as in Sicily or in the Robin Hood legend has been interpreted as a form of class warfare. Crowd actions or riots, such as ghetto reactions to police brutality or other violations of the expectations of residents, have also been interpreted as symbolic expressions of class consciousness. The Watergate conspiracy, in contrast, has been interpreted by contemporary Marxist thinkers (Marcuse, 1973) as an effort to consolidate power in the face of a worsening situation in the world market system and loss of control of the economies of developing countries, such as Vietnam and Cambodia. The conspirators in the White House attempted to discipline those elements in the United States who questioned the policy of support for corrupt and conservative governments in Indochina. Efforts to harass and weaken the Democratic Party were also undertaken as a way of consolidating control over critics who voiced opposition to the policy to continue the high rate of return for investments despite growing competition from producers outside the United States.

Although very rigid Marxist interpretations of deviance are no longer frequently encountered in American and Western European sociology, a strong Marxist influence is found in almost all variations of conflict theories and is combined by many with labeling and other theoretical approaches.

Conflicts of Cultures and Norms

In the United States, several schools of thought have placed the concept of conflict at the center of their theoretical focus. Anomie is a theory of conflict not simply between means and ends but between those who are able to utilize legitimate means to gain access to socially approved goals and those who resort to other mechanisms because opportunities to reach these goals by normative paths are blocked. Anomie thus explains the emergence of the conflict envisaged by the Marxists as essentially one produced by the limitations on opportunity for many people. Several early adherents of labeling, particularly Frank Tannenbaum (1938), projected an image of deviant behavior as arising out of a clash of forces in society. Children and adolescents are counterpoised to authority figures in school, at home, and on the street; the children are sometimes driven to defend themselves against these others, and then the hostile, authoritarian, and punitive reaction (an entirely unnecessary overreaction in many instances) compels many such youth to shift toward more antisocial forms of behavior. They become what they were accused (or suspected) of being.

The conflict theme is apparent in the work of Edwin Lemert (1964), who, in his critique of anomie theory, questioned the assumption of a value consensus in America and pointed out the variety of acts that are considered proper in some ethnic groups but objectionable, even illegal, in others. John Lofland (1969) suggested that deviance could best be understood as an identity that emerges in conflict between groups or between an individual and the groups around him; and R. D. Laing saw many forms of schizophrenia as defenses in a conflict situation, particularly within a family. The idea of neuroses as defensive adjustments can be found in Freud and other early psychoanalytic writers.

In 1931, several decades before the advent of the concept of socially assigned deviant identities, Louis Wirth (1964 ed.) drew attention to the effect of migration on misconduct and the problem of adapting to new norms:

> Most human beings, living in a civilization akin to our own, are exposed to experiences that carry back to varied cultural settings. To understand their problems of adjustment, therefore, it is necessary to view the personalities from the perspective of their cultural matrix and to note the contradictions, the inconsistencies, and the incongruities of the cultural influences that impinge upon them. The hypothesis may be set forth that the physical and psy-

chic tensions which express themselves in attitudes and in overt conduct may be correlated with culture conflicts. This hypothesis may, to be sure, not always prove fitting.

Wirth found that culture conflicts were not confined to immigrant families but occurred in other families and communities as well, "especially where, as is the case in city life, contacts are extended, heterogeneous groups mingle, neighborhoods disappear, and people, deprived of local and family ties, are forced to live under the loose, transient, and impersonal relations that are characteristic of cities." He warned that culture conflict was but one factor in the understanding of misconduct and that by stressing it he was not disputing but merely neglecting all others. In a culture-conflict situation, Wirth believed, the person accused of misconduct often behaves in a manner that appears proper to himself:

> Our conduct, whatever it may consist of, or however it might be judged by the world at large, appears genuinely moral to us when we can get the people whom we regard as significant in our social world to accept and approve it. One of the most convincing bits of evidence for the importance of the role played by culture conflict in the cases that have come to my attention is the frequency with which delinquents, far from exhibiting a sense of guilt, made the charge of hypocrisy toward official representatives of the social order such as teachers, judges, newspapers, and social workers with whom they came in contact.

Expanding on Wirth's study of some human migration, Thorsten Sellin (1938) proposed that culture conflict, particularly the conflict of norms between various ethnic groups, could be understood as a major explanation of crime. Modern societies (and this is especially true of the United States) no longer have any semblance of homogeneity. It is not class conflict that is the foremost theme in understanding the behavior of transgressors, but the fact that people who do not accept each other's styles of living today reside, if not side by side, then in the same cities and certainly the same countries. Wars, colonial exploitation, slavery, enforced and voluntary migrations, national disasters (such as famine), escape from dictatorship and tyranny—all have caused people of different ancestries, having dissimilar physical characteristics, sometimes speaking different languages, and with dissimilar religious beliefs and practices to become neighbors and citizens of the same country. Geographic mobility has been accelerated and facilitated by ease and rapidity of travel (and, in addition, migration has become reversible). Industrialization and urbanization, those two great forces that (perhaps with secularism and bureaucratization) have been dominant social factors in determining life patterns in the second half of the twentieth century, have resulted in these people seeing one another in factories, in stores, at union meetings, on streets, and in schools; whereas, in an earlier period, with a larger rural and agricultural populace and much more difficulty in traveling, people of diverse origins commingled only infrequently.

For Sellin, these groups—mainly racial, religious, or of different national origins—brought to each other and to their new land a variety of beliefs about what constituted appropriate behavior. What was right within their own group was abhorrent, even criminal, in the eyes of others, or to the dominant Anglo-American culture of the United States.

It appears (although these figures are difficult to validate and are open to different explanations) that the crime rate was greater among immigrants than among comparable people in the native country from which they had departed. Of course, there may have been selectivity here. The rate in a European country, or in a given class in that country, might be low, but those who were least adjusted to the normative life or most likely to get into trouble with the law might be the most likely to leave. This is conjectural and does not suggest that they were "shipped out" and exiled to become pioneers as punishment for their crimes, although that is indeed what occurred in the colonization of Australia by the British.

Further, it may have been that disappointments arising from the struggle for existence in a land whose streets one expected to be paved with gold or where one believed many people to be opulent led some immigrants into criminal paths. Nor would labeling perspectives here be devoid of value, for the newcomers were ridiculed and despised, given few opportunities, treated as inferiors, and some of them no doubt became what they were defined as being and thus were expected to be.

Sellin sought to account for such criminality as was encountered in a dynamic society in terms of a conflict of norms. A conduct norm, he suggested, may be regarded "as a rule supported by sanctions which reflect the value attached to the norm by the normative group. . . . The severest sanctions everywhere are those which deprive the nonconformist of rights, privileges and benefits which are most treasured by the group and which the conformist may enjoy." While Sellin's greatest interest was in the violation of legal norms or the commission of crimes, it is clear from this formulation that there are strong informal sanctions that would penalize the nonconformist by depriving him of rights, privileges, or benefits most treasured by the group.

Culture conflicts can also arise within a single society. There are endogenous conflicts that may be brought forth by technology, for instance. Kingsley Davis (1940) has suggested, in fact, that intergenerational conflict is directly related to the rate of social and technological change; that is, parents are in conflict with their children because they are still guided by the norms of twenty years earlier and hence see their children's behavior as incomprehensible or immoral, although the children are acting normatively from their generation's viewpoint. This thesis has been extended considerably by Margaret Mead (1965) and then popularized by Alvin Toffler (1970). But for the United States and most of the rest of the twentieth-century world, culture conflicts were of exogenous origin. They were conflicts of cultural codes. While the rural migrants to the city might still behave in the fashion of the countryside, Sellin felt that this was a relatively minor source of abrasion, as he assumed that they had absorbed the basic norms of the entire culture, comprising as it does both town and country.

Culture conflict takes place when two groups having clashing codes live in contiguous areas, when there is migration, or when the law of one group is extended to cover the other. Anthropologists have noted that murder for revenge has been not only permitted but encouraged in some groups; these acts became major crimes, however, when the law of a European country was imposed on a formerly independent tribe. Polygyny, various forms of sexual conduct, exhibition of the unveiled face by women, and the murder by parents of their daughter's seducer —these are examples of behaviors that are crimes among some people and normative expectations among others.

But it is not only when people relocate in another society that conflict arises; as Sellin (1938:63) points out, the norms themselves may move:

> Conflicts of cultures are inevitable when the norms of one cultural or subcultural area migrate to or come in contact with those of another, and it is interesting to note that most of the specific researches on culture conflict and delinquency have been concerned with this aspect of conflict.

Thus, the conflict involves divergent codes of conduct held to by different groups, not necessarily the people who have internalized these clashing and irreconcilable codes.

One might expect culture conflict to lend itself to empirical confirmation, particularly as it applies to crime if not to other forms of deviance, or at least as it is applied to specific aspects of disvalued behavior, such as alcoholism or prostitution, that are found in many societies. The problem of such confirmation is formidable in the extreme, but most studies seem to point in the direction of lesser crime, not greater, for migrant groups than for the natives in the same area. Franco Ferracuti (1968) made a study of all reports and researches of this phenomenon in Europe, noted the relatively greater or lesser reliability of the work, and showed that whereas Irish immigrants in England had more brushes with the law than did the English, the reverse was true of Italian migrant workers in Switzerland and many other groups. Israel would seem to be an ideal testing spot for the Sellin theory, as it is largely a nation of immigrants and children of immigrants, and there are diverse groups in close contact with one another, in the European Jewish population, the North African Jews, Oriental Jews, and Arabs, among others. Shlomo Shoham (1966) studied juvenile delinquency and crime rates for these various groups, and at first glance these data would appear to validate the conflict thesis. However, the North African immigrants, he points out, had been in relatively better status positions before migration, and many were faced with poor housing and other disappointments on arrival in Israel. This loss of status may motivate people to try new, nonapproved ways of regaining their former power, privileges, and prestige.

There are complexities in studying this problem that could lead to unwarranted exaggeration in either of two directions. One might underestimate the amount of deviance among inigrants because some groups, in "taking care of their own," handle transgressions as internal matters and conceal them from the authorities. This practice, which arises from the desire to project a more favorable image to those whose acceptance they seek and from the ease with which it can be accomplished, has taken place among Orientals in almost all lands in which they settled, and among Eastern European and Mediterranean Jews in Western Europe and North America. In other instances, authorities tended to overlook the transgressions in which members of the migrant group were themselves victims, a phenomenon not infrequent in the Spanish-speaking ghettoes of the United States.

These would diminish the amount of recorded deviance, but other factors outweigh those already described. Members of a socially outcast group are afforded fewer opportunities for jobs and housing and are usually of a lower social class. They are more frequently suspected and more often found guilty, and their acts are remembered by the public that "knows" that these people are no good.

The greatest difficulty with the culture-conflict theory as one looks closely at it and challenges its precepts is that it is validated by exceptional circumstances, not by ordinary criminal and deviant behavior. One hears of the Sicilian father acquitted of murdering the youth who seduced his daughter. But culture-conflict theorists seldom discuss theft, that most pervasive of delicts, which is not sanctioned anywhere (except when it is perpetrated by the power group against a victimized population, as in colonial lands). Most murders and assaults, it would appear, cannot be explained by a narrow theory of conflict of conduct norms arising out of migration, whether of peoples or their values. Sexual practices differ from place to place, but few manifestations of sexual deviance are explicable in terms of Sellin's framework. Certainly the drinking of alcoholic beverages in some denominations is religiously proscribed and in others (for example, Mormons) limited but religiously prescribed. But this does not account for the five million alcoholics estimated to live in the United States. One can cite the American Indian groups that use peyote regularly in their religious rites and some Orientals for whom opium smoking was acceptable, but this is irrelevant to the American drug scene, just as primitive ritual infanticide or adult-child sexual intercourse has nothing to do with child slaying or the statutory rape of a five-year-old as these occur in the Western world.

Far from believing that the acts they perform and for which they are apprehended and punished are proper, many delinquents, in the view of David Matza (1964), accept the values of the culture whose norms they have violated. They are not self-righteous; one might say that they are "self-wrongeous."

The casting of deviance into a framework of social conflict is a central theme in the work of Lofland (1969:13–14):

> The defining of persons and acts as deviant can be seen as a particular instance of generalized ways in which social organization and social definition can differ. At the level of a single and *total society*, such a basis is found in the dynamics of what proportion of a society, how well organized and how powerful, are *fearful* of, and feel *threatened* by, some other portion of the society. Organized social life can be viewed as a game in which actors and collectivities defend themselves against distrusted and suspected others. . . .
>
> Under different levels of fear, size, organization and power between parties in conflict, there are corresponding changes in public definitions of the situation. Persons and acts in a small, powerless minority that are at one time regarded as merely deviant may, at another time, be felt to constitute a civil uprising, social movement or civil war. Theft, arson, assault, torture and murder perpetrated by individuals is simply deviance; when perpetrated by a loosely organized minority acting in concert such acts might be imputed to have a political meaning, and, when performed in the context of a civil or revolutionary war—that is, by a well organized minority—they are acts of war or of liberation or legitimate defense. [Italics in original.]

Conflict and the Heterogeneous Society

The culture-conflict theory is powerful, but it has by and large been imprisoned in the framework in which it was originally presented (not to deny that several critics have suggested that it can be developed far beyond its early form). It is too narrow in its focus on a conflict of conduct norms rather than of people in a heterogeneous society, in its focus on crime rather than on deviance in its noncriminal aspects, and in the attention it gives to immigrants rather than to diverse peoples in conflict with each other.

Migrant groups, including the internal migrants of lower social class and those separated by race, language, or strong traditions, are seldom accepted by the host society in which they settle. They are often ghettoized, feel (rightly or wrongly) that they are ill-treated, are offered smaller opportunities, and have deep resentments against the world around them. The migration may result in a weakening of family bonds without substitution of new forces of control that they can respect. They are catapulted into class conflict, on the one hand, and race and ethnic conflict, on the other. They see the world through the eyes of the oppressed, and their acts of anger and hostility are cries (and crimes) of despair. Out of the antagonisms between the old and the new peoples emerges a subculture in which transgression and depredation, and sometimes degradation, thrive. It is a conflict, in short, of peoples and cultures more than of norms and values.

Further, the conflict may explain why some acts are seen as deviant by outsiders but acceptable by insiders, and this is closer to the conduct-norm approach than when one looks at the vengeful father committing murder. In American society, it would appear that black groups accepted premarital sexual behavior before many white groups did, and the girl who had relinquished her virginity at a relatively early age was not considered "loose" or "bad," although white people continued for many decades to make that judgment. Illegitimacy was less highly stigmatized at the time among blacks than among whites. Similarly, gambling practices differ in various subcultures. For years, people in America ridiculed those who were carrying out certain religious rituals that were visible but not criminal. Even speaking with a foreign accent has been subject to sarcastic barbs from members of the society who were not on the level of those they called "green-horns."

Finally, the conflicts in a heterogeneous society are more than those between ethnic, racial, religious, and immigrant or migrant groups and the norm-giving majority. They are more than the class conflicts that Marxists have elevated to a central position in their image of the world in upheaval. They are age-group struggles, political and other life-style clashes, and strife among numerous subcultural groups. Some of these arise out of a deviation (or what is defined as deviance), such as conflicts between homosexuals, organized or not, and the rest of society, or between parents of the retarded and the medical and helping professions. Teenagers are in sharp conflict with school, family, and other sources of authority, and it is in the course of this struggle that they are likely to be pushed toward greater differentiation of themselves from the controlling and norm-defining people.

Some of this heterogeneity is inevitable in a society that gives differential privileges and opportunities to persons of various age, sex, and other groups, but it is accentuated in a fast-changing world; it is brought to the fore by the developments of urbanization as large numbers of similarly situated persons are in contact with one another and with dissimilar persons. Finally, heterogeneity is made into a central fact of life by the coterminous existence of racial, ethnic, migrant, and other social groups, whose struggles for survival in the urban centers suggest a framework of conflict, protest, and dissension that becomes endemic in the society.

5

Society's Reaction

SOCIETY AGAINST DEVIANTS

There are many ways in which society can deal with deviants. One method is for it to change itself; another is for it to urge the deviants to undergo change. It is only when change takes place, whether in social attitudes or behavior patterns, that the social problem posed by an aspect of deviance can be said to have been solved. This can take the form of complete acceptance where formerly there was hostility; one can see this occurring in America with regard to nonmarital cohabitation, and some people are struggling for a change in this direction vis-à-vis homosexuality. Or the modification can take place in the deviant, by either renunciation or rehabilitation, whichever is the more fitting. Less complete than either of these would be what might be termed *accommodation:* a mutual tolerance (or, more precisely, a tolerance by the normals of the deviants), a muted hostility cloaked in the language and mannerisms of good taste—something short of acceptance but not quite what can be termed *oppression.* On the receiving end of this accommodation is the deviant, accepting the limited opportunities that exist and learning to live with them.

A great deal of emphasis has been placed on the official societal reaction to deviance. It is much easier to see, comprehend, measure, and describe than the unofficial reactions that are not buttressed by law, codified, and handled through institutions and agencies of social control. However, there is a considerable tradition in American sociology that is concerned with symbolic meanings, gestures, cues, and other subtle forms of communication used to convey approval or disapproval to others.

The heavy burden of guilt and shame that people carry is often not for fear of punishment if one is apprehended for having done wrong. Rather, it derives from a horror of being disapproved of by others, particularly by meaningful or significant others, and from the fact that the values of these others have often been accepted by the rule-breaker. Charles Cooley worked with the concept of a "looking-glass self," the notion that each person develops an image of himself as he sees himself being seen by others; that is, the eyes of others constitute a mirror in which he sees his own image and makes judgments of it. Normative behavior would be understood not only in terms of avoidance of official punishment or governmental sanctions and the gaining of official rewards (jobs, promotions, invitations, and the like) but also as avoidance of feeling that one has been negatively judged and, from this, is compelled to judge oneself negatively.

The unofficial mechanisms for the punishment of the deviant range from overt and blatant exclusion to subtle patronization. They include the raised eyebrow, the wink, the slight sneering smile, the tacit communication to another, "Let's be tolerant; we know what the score is." Overt expression of contempt is often suppressed, but the victim is given to know that it is there, that he is not a whole person in the sense that someone else is, that in fact everyone else is, including those who have other shortcomings and defects which are not reacted to negatively.

Language strongly expresses social hostility, reflecting the aura of a society showing contempt for its deviants. The vocabulary of ethnic slurs, for example, includes even words of contempt for those who do not uphold in-group loyalty, as when white liberals are called "nigger lovers" or accommodating black people "Uncle Toms." The scorn in which homosexuals are held is likewise illustrated by a rich vocabulary: from so guarded a reference as "one of them" to the overt "screaming fag." It is an indication of standards of normative behavior against which feminists have protested that males have an arsenal of scornful terms not only for females who are sexually promiscuous ("whore") but even for those who are permissive ("easy lay," "pushover," and others).

Humor is used to express the putdown that characterizes the attitude toward deviants. Probably no group has been subjected to more systematic humiliation through humor than the American black people, and it is all the more important that this was reflected in the world of respectable Americans; for example, in after-dinner jokes at meetings of "scholars" and of political, labor, business, and community leaders. This antiblack humor is chronicled in American art, journalism, and scholarship, starting at the time of the colonies and disappearing for all practical purposes or going underground at about the time of World War II.

Few mechanisms against the deviant are more widely used than social exclusion. While there are many criteria for deciding who should and who should not be made a part of a private or inner group, when a person is systematically excluded and he has a given characteristic, he is likely to believe (or to want to believe) that that characteristic is responsible for the exclusion. True, one may be denied the invitation, the job, or the proposal of marriage for an entirely different reason. But those who have received such rebuffs regularly and who have watched others, presumably less qualified, passing muster while no one with traits like their own does so, are unlikely to be able to blame anything but discriminatory practices.

Exclusion takes the form of oversolicitous efforts to avoid being the excluder or, at least, having one's exclusionary actions become known. There is here a presumed sensitivity to the feelings of others, as seen in seating arrangements on a public vehicle. The first seats to be occupied are almost always lone seats, usually next to a window, and the adjacent seat will be occupied only if the window occupant is accompanied by another person. Then, when all the lone seats have been taken, those entering alone must choose. If a white person enters, he must choose a white companion, and the black must choose a black, for fear of violating the rules governing exclusion and excluded. But a white person may deliberately go forward with just such a violation, in order to express his freedom from the prejudice that characterizes the black as deviant, but in so doing he is actually expressing his realization that the prejudice exists. For the black person, the options are even more restricted.

Rebuke is the mechanism frequently used for handling children who have overstepped the bounds of propriety. With children, however, it is a learning process. The rebuke is part of a system of punishments and rewards; it is a mild punishment, telling the child that the behavior is unacceptable and that other activity is expected and will be welcomed. Thus, the rebuke teaches as well as corrects; one might say that it corrects by teaching as much as by punishing.

When the same type of rebuke is given to an adult, it is meant to be purely punitive. One does not seek to bring the adult into the orbit of acceptability and often respectability; instead, one communicates by the rebuke that not only the act is reprehensible but so is the person committing it.

In some instances, the exclusion is leveled solely against the activity, not against the perpetrator. This is frequently so with adultery, for example, but almost never with other forms of sexually disapproved actions, such as child molestation, rape, or homosexuality. Adultery in this way is defined as being socially undesirable and to be avoided, but as within the orbit of activities performed by otherwise normal, decent, and law-abiding persons.

It is sometimes stated that people cannot be forced to like others or to socialize with them if they do not like them. People will choose their friends, even as they will choose their mates. But in the case of deviance, they exclude others from the friendship circle and the marriage reservoir not only for themselves but for friends and family as well. They express disapproval not only of a relationship but of the person entering into it.

When the deviant is subjected to official handling and treatment by power groups in society, it appears that his difficulties derive from legal and other official sanctions. Oppression, however, is not necessarily legal and can be the more burdensome as it becomes difficult to pinpoint, as it conceals itself behind façades and pretends to be what it is not. While it is difficult to imagine any oppression that can equal the extermination, genocide, and enslavement of American blacks and Indians, Armenian nationals during the rule of the Turks, and Jews in Europe from 1933 to 1945, there is a very real oppression that expresses itself in terms of contempt, inequality of opportunity, and downgrading of the person. Victims have been those afflicted with epilepsy or leprosy, the mentally retarded, the insane, blacks, homosexuals—in short, deviants. Those who are conceptualized as capable of responsibility for their actions and statuses are, by some curious irony, actually better regarded, not worse, by their brethren. This may be because there is hope: because they are in control of their fate, they may become reasonable and see the light, deciding that their moral failing need not continue. Thus, it is easier to think in terms of rehabilitation for the bank robber than for the former mental patient; the latter has a permanent and ineffaceable mark, branded by a society that believes, of some things: If once, then always.

One of the ways of demonstrating that a status is downgraded is that the status is used in place of the person: she is a "pushover," one says, but there is no common analogous term for the sex-hungry male precisely because "stud" is a term of approval. The replacement of the individual by the category with which he is identified, the failure to see the person as a person, has been viewed as the touchstone of the minority group. It is the ultimate in depersonalization and hence in dehumanization. In terms of the deviant, it occurs only when his deviance occupies a master status that takes precedence over all his other statuses: no matter what roles such a person occupies, he does so as, for example, a black or a homosexual. "Former mental patient" is another category invested with master status; no matter what such a person achieves, for good or ill, it is the achievement, accomplishment, or dereliction of one who has been institutionalized for mental illness.

Agencies of Control

When one speaks of agencies of social control, one is usually referring to governmental bodies—the police, the courts, or perhaps some youth board or authority. However, agencies of control can be organized and quasi-official without being quite governmental, as a social-welfare office or a charitable organization. Finally, there are powerful social-control agents with no official or semi-official status, as friends, peers, neighbors, significant and even not very significant others.

If one defines deviance in terms of patterned activities that arouse stigmatization, indignation, horror, abhorrence, antipathy, or some similar reaction among the general public, then unofficial and popular attitudes toward the transgressor, or negative definitions of him, must be considered powerful forces. These are the factors that contribute so largely to an individual's sense of shame and guilt and to his viewing himself as inferior in some important respect. It is not to deny the force and effect of a policeman with gun in hand to emphasize that this is only one way of instilling in an individual the sense that he is one of society's rejects.

The mechanism by which informal control operates and its effects on the deviant have been studied less frequently than that of formal control. It is relatively easy, for example, to see how social class will help to determine whether a youth is sent home with an apology from the judge or whether, for the same offense, he finds himself in prison. It is not quite so simple to determine the social-class factors in informal rejection. There are clues, but they are hard to quantify. We might conclude that acceptance of the deviant seems to increase as one goes up in the class scale while painful slurs and rejecting attitudes appear to be muted. Acceptance, in short, seems to be greater with higher social class, but at the same time it is enshrouded in circumspection.

Formal sanctions affect the official label. However, there is an unofficial label—when, for example, everybody knows because "Big Mouth" was talking on the block—that can be just as oppressive and more difficult to combat. The informal, above all, may have a severe effect on the personality formation of the deviant and his day-to-day activities. It plays a significant part in his decisions about the strategy to be used in managing his "spoiled identity" (Goffman, 1963)—the feeling that he is not looked upon by others as being a good, moral, decent, or whole person but bears a mark, brand, or stigma—and in navigating not just during the daily events but for his entire life.

Hostility can be overtly or subtly manifested. When it is not evident to the offender, it may be to others, which the transgressor learns about in a variety of ways. It takes the forms of ridicule, sneering, scorn, snickering, gossip, mimic and parody, exclusion from certain functions to which one is otherwise eligible, discrimination in jobs or in other capacities, name-calling, slurs, and forthright denunciation. It is expressed in the area of sociability, and particularly in opportunities for courtship and marriage, and it communicates not only that what one does (or is) is disvalued but that people are doing something about it—making fun, acting out, ridiculing, excluding.

The snicker and the stare come to be so expected by some highly visible deviants that they impute meaning even to laughter unrelated to a given situation or to fleeting eye contact, caught or imagined. Under these conditions, the deviant often comes to resent onlookers. His reaction may be to make his disvalued characteristic even more obvious; to scorn those who scorn him; to retort in kind and in anger, staring back hard and fast.

Such a deviant lives in constant fear of gossip, knowing or imagining that it is going on around him. On a superficial level, one can say that gossip is not very dangerous. It cannot cause imprisonment or, usually, impoverishment (although the deviant may bear a heavy economic burden because of job discrimination). But gossip reduces him to a person who is talked about. The celebrity can ignore this or perhaps turn it into an advantage ("I'll cry all the way to the bank"), but not so the ordinary man or woman.

It is in the social arena that the deviant meets the greatest rejection, and unless he joins forces with others who are like himself or who have some other deviant characteristic, he may go so far as to retreat into almost complete isolation.

Humor and Social Control

Humor is a two-sided weapon; it can be used not only to subject people to ridicule but also to disarm those who are likely to be uncomfortable in the presence of the deviant. It makes light of tragedy, brings the unmentionable into the forefront of con-

versation, and, in short, permits the heavy air of embarrassment
to be lifted. Anatole Broyard (1950), writing about racial stereo-
types, termed this *minstrelization:*

> Minstrelization takes innumerable forms, in each case involving
> the Negro's willing capitulation to the anti-Negro's definition of
> him. A subtle example is the attribution of inherent greater
> "rhythmicality" to the Negro, and the inauthentic Negro's accep-
> tance of this alleged trait, which is taken to show, of course, that
> the Negro is a more primitive creature, more animal-like, not yet
> emancipated by the short-circuiting effects of full consciousness
> from the primeval earth-throb.

What is involved here is a deliberate impersonation of the
stereotype in mockery of oneself. In the words of Erving Goffman
(1963), "The stigmatized person ingratiatingly acts out before
normals the full dance of bad qualities imputed to his kind,
thereby consolidating a life situation into a clownish role."

But it doesn't always work. An extremely short young adult,
invited to a friend's home for dinner, asks if there is a high chair
for him when he sits down to eat. Such a remark may reduce the
tension by suggesting that the guest knows that people are thinking about his size and wants to let them know that it is not
unmentionable; but his mention of it at the same time may accen-
tuate the tension by embarrassing the hosts, who do not have an
acceptable response in their available repertoire. Further, minstrelization played out by a black man, or by an effeminate male,
may be a sharp though subtle manner of showing contempt for
the normal who holds the stereotype, a mechanism for ridiculing
not the stereotype but those who believe in it. The deviant is here
a sort of double agent. For the physically disabled, this usage of
the role of clown is not appealing, although sometimes it is used
for financial advantage, as in a circus. Most people with spoiled
identities are too sensitive about the defect to be able to handle
it in this manner. Again, it is something that only a celebrity, or
one with other strong compensatory features, can cope with.
Self-mockery, however, is not to be confused with the use of
humor by normals to subject others to ridicule. The latter, in fact,
is a major weapon by which a society makes certain of its norma-

tive requirements known to its members. It is especially damaging to the secret deviant, who must often join in laughter directed at himself.

Control through Collective Behavior

Informal negative sanctions can best be understood as social devices for maintaining solidarity among the conforming members of society; that is, for keeping them from getting out of line. In addition to sneers, ostracism, and ridicule, informal social control takes another form: the rule of the mob, or even of an individual or a small group, who decide, unauthorized by law, to inflict punishment on another—to kill him, hold him captive, run him out of town, put him out of business, or perhaps place illegal pressure on public officials to punish him. This type of informal sanction is often invoked with the connivance of public officials, in which case it can be said to be institutionalized and quasi-official public policy; or it can be done with no official approval or connivance, in which instance it takes the form of criminal acts, although seldom prosecuted as such.

Informal sanctions are forms of rewards and punishments (mainly the latter), warning against behavior that will bring rejection by society. The aim is to strengthen the moral stance of the normals, infusing them with a sense of correctness, well-being, and uprightness as they join other good, whole, and normal people in heaping ridicule on the outcast. One may argue, as Kai Erikson (1966) has done, that society needs its deviants to promote solidarity and belief in the efficacy and power of its rules. Those who might otherwise stray are thus warned to keep their place.

In some instances, informality acts to supplement the official reaction, infusing it with public support and leaving the transgressor almost alone and friendless. An extreme example is the convicted spy who is despised by his fellow-prisoners, so heinous in their eyes was his crime. Without support by some informal sanctions, the formal rules tend to be rather ineffective, although strong government-sponsored propaganda can combat this. But it is with regard to matters that are not the business of the law but matters of state that social control operates through strong yet unofficial sanctions. It has often been contended that tsarist governments provoked attacks by the peasants upon the Jewish communities as a way of diverting the attention of the impoverished from the government's ineptitude and incapacity to modernize Russia; and that attacks by poor whites on the black communities of the South had similar functions, namely, to divert attention from the extreme poverty of both blacks and whites.

Those subject to informal sanctions are particularly helpless, for they often live without an enemy they can engage. Even when aware of the source and reason for the hostility, the deviant continues to be a helpless victim, for to defend himself and counterattack might only produce greater difficulties. He cannot establish his innocence before a judge and jury, for no one has accused him; informal sanctions are punishments without accusation or indictment. And if he does place himself before an official body that finds him innocent, he may still be subject to the rebukes of peers, friends, family, and neighbors, whose judgments are not affected by an official exoneration.

Informal control may take on the form of muted hostility. This occurs when the anger against the transgressor is for some reason unable to gain open expression. Max Scheler (1961 ed.) has described this process (although he did not apply it to hostility toward those who violate group norms) under the concept of *ressentiment,* defined as "an attitude which arises from a cumulative repression of feelings of hatred, revenge, envy and the like."

The Gamble of Living

In the end, social living is a gamble. Each step in one's daily pace through life is an exposure to which the deviant is highly vulnerable. Much energy is expended avoiding, responding to, or defending oneself against rejection. Perhaps it can be summarized in the situation of the pregnant unmarried girl. She hides her protruding belly as long as possible with tight girdle and loose coat, and she feels the sting of neighbors who turn and look. She even feels the rebuke of those who do not turn but who, she believes, must be staring at her as she passes them on the street. She raises her head higher than others, because she feels it is falling lower. Finally, she moves, changes her name or puts "Mrs." in front of it, and takes on the biography of a widow or a divorcée. Few believe her, but a new game is being played, and the rules of informal sanctions are now cloaked in silence and mutual make-believe.

Sanctions are needed to the extent that rules are required but not accepted as the best and most natural way of doing things by all members of society. For some rules, it is possible to tolerate both the rule and its transgressor. Heaping ridicule upon the latter is a cruel but usually effective means of enjoining people from doing what powerful others do not want them to do, but it results in an unnecessary amount of suffering for those who cannot or will not keep in line.

For the involuntary deviant, informal sanctions appear to be meaningless. They cannot control him. They cannot get him back in line. They do, however, reaffirm the standard of the group; they glorify beauty, health, youth, strength, and physical and mental perfection. That this can be accomplished without ridicule and ostracism seems apparent, but it is not a road that people in all societies often choose.

Social Hostility as Amplification of Deviance—The Perspective of Labeling

Traditionally, the fact that society reacted, officially and unofficially, in a hostile way against norm violators was assumed to be inevitable, necessary, and desirable. Punishment would deter, correct, or at least motivate people to control their urges to conduct themselves in a way that others saw as sinful, immoral, or hurtful. And punishment, as Emile Durkheim conceived it, serves to isolate the transgressor, to reinforce the norms that others obey, and to unite these others in a cohesive society of law-abiding people.

This view of the social usefulness of hostility has been challenged by many commentators on the racial scene, particularly Merton (1948). For example, if people are thought of as uneducable, Merton argued, and are given few if any educational opportunities, they will become what they were originally (*and falsely*) believed to be—thus, the self-fulfilling prophecy.

The application of this concept to deviance has roots that go back many centuries but became particularly popular in the 1960s with the development of a school of thought, a perspective, known as *labeling*. Its first modern theoretical application to norm violators seems to have been in a work by Frank Tannenbaum, who in 1938 wrote of mischievous youths who are tagged delinquent, who are made into criminals (which they were not in the first place) by a process of "tagging, defining, segregating, describing, emphasizing," until "the person becomes the thing he is described as being."

Later, in 1951, Edwin Lemert published an influential book, *Social Pathology*, in which he suggested that things are not intrinsically good or evil but only become so by the way they are seen and reacted to in society. When deviation is reacted to in a hostile manner, two things occur, one official and one unofficial, that aggravate an already difficult situation. First, the perpetrator is labeled by others as a deviator, an evil or abnormal person, not to be trusted and not to be admitted into the world of humanity with ordinary, law-abiding, good folk. Second, as a result of how people are labeled and reacted to, they develop defenses, fears, paranoia, mental anguish, low self-image, or self-hate, all of which result in a new and secondary form of deviation. This secondary deviation is infinitely more harmful than the relatively mild deviance for which they had originally been labeled.

After Lemert, the outstanding proponent of the labeling perspective was Howard S. Becker, whose work *Outsiders: Studies in the Sociology of Deviance* (1963) gave the study of the socially disapproved and rejected intellectual excitement by placing major emphasis on the hostile social reaction as the deviance-creating force. In Becker's view, deviance is created by those in society who make the rules whose infraction constitutes the disapproved behavior, and then selectively apply these rules to some persons but not to others.

Outsiders was not merely a theoretical contribution to the study of disvalued people; it was indeed a manifesto, and around its formulations arose what came close to becoming, within sociology, a social movement.

The Act of Placing a Label

Man is a language-using animal. In the nature of language, he divides inanimate objects, people, thoughts, acts, or any other type of things into groups, categories, or classes, including some objects with others because they have a characteristic in common, although they are dissimilar in an infinite variety of ways. In order to speak and write about these groups of things that are alike in some respect, he places a label (a tag, name, or counter) on them.

There are several meanings that can be imputed to the process of labeling, and sometimes it is not entirely clear from the literature which is meant by scholars using this perspective in the study of deviance. Labeling may refer to any of the following acts (and possibly many more):

1. The placement of a person within a category: male or female, student or professor, athlete or diabetic, or whatever. This is a necessary and inevitable process and in and of itself may have no consequences pertinent to antisocial or rejected behavior.

2. The attribution of negative status to the category, as is the case when the label is prostitute, alcoholic, cripple, dope fiend, and many others.

3. The identification of someone as belonging in a negative group, as by retrospective definition: the processes by which this takes place, the cues that are picked up and the clues that are pursued, important in the case of secret deviance (Kitsuse, 1962).

4. The differential application of the label (and the consequences of that differential application) to persons of different social class, education, race, and influence. The literature on juvenile delinquency is particularly rich in material of this nature, as is the literature on race and crime.

5. The employment of the specific word *deviant,* or its many synonyms, to describe either an individual or a group of persons.

6. The arbitrary choice of a label for an individual or category, to express and evoke diverse quantities and qualities of hostility; as, for example, whore, slut, prostitute, courtesan, call girl, harlot, pushover, or loose woman, all without regard to the subtle and gross differences that could be drawn between these categories.

7. The pejorative use of a label as an epithet, often without regard to the content of the ideas or the character of the acts. This is the manner in which such terms as, for instance, sexist, racist, Red or communist, fascist, middle class, and whore are at times used.

The Essentials of Labeling

No one speaks for labeling; each writer speaks for himself. One can find quotes among the works of various authorities showing that labeling does (or does not) take into account the idiosyncracies of the individual actor, does (or does not) accept the concept of the unapprehended as being deviant. It appears that some adherents of labeling see no acts as inherently evil; yet elsewhere this is contradicted.

Nevertheless, it may be said that there is general agreement that the following themes are central to the labeling perspective:

1. Actions derive their characteristic of "badness," not from their intrinsic content, but from the way in which they are defined by others, particularly by the rule-makers and rule-abiders in a society.

2. It is not especially useful to look at the nature of the act or the characteristics of the actor in order to understand the phenomenon of deviance; rather, one must examine the nature of the condemning society and the process by which some people gain the power and ascendancy to successfully place the label of deviant on others.

3. The process of placing the label of deviant, and of reacting to the individual as a transgressor, varies not only with the nature of the act but also with who the transgressor is. Official and unofficial reaction to deviance is not predictable from the act itself but varies according to social class and power relationships.

4. As a result of the official societal reaction to a person as a deviant, he is processed and handled as such. The label of deviant (more frequently a label embodying the negative character of deviance without that word) is placed on him, and this usually results in new, secondary deviance that is more severe and more damaging to society than the original act. Further, the placing of

this label and the public identification of the individual as deviant reinforces or "fixes" the individual in that status.

5. By virtue of the "master status" potential of deviance, there are careers or stages in the development of the deviant, as in other roles and in occupations. These careers are facilitated by the official reaction to persons as deviant, particularly by their exclusion from the society of normals and their incarceration with others who have been cast out by society.

In short, for the labelists, deviance is manufactured by the hostile reaction of rule-makers. Not all rule-breakers are reacted to in a hostile manner, it depends on who they are, what they do, and to some extent on the visibility of the act. Breaking a rule, therefore, is not enough to establish a deviant role or identity. If society did not manufacture deviance, it would not exist. Furthermore, the label perpetuates and aggravates the deviance.

Problems with the Labeling Approach

The labeling perspective has been staunchly defended and frequently opposed. There are several major criticisms that have been offered:

The problem of limited applicability. General statements are often made regarding the applicability of labeling to all forms of deviance, but it is interesting that few efforts have been made to study and understand ordinary crime (particularly violent crime and property crime) from this perspective. Richard Quinney (1970) and Clayton Hartjen (1974) have attempted to extend labeling to "ordinary crime," but most labeling work is much more limited.

Nonetheless, this is not primarily an argument against labeling but merely a statement that it might have to be confined to certain types of deviance. It is possible that the perspective may explain a great deal about homosexuality or juvenile delinquency, for example, but little about rape; that it may tell us a good deal about marijuana use but little about armed robbery (except when it is performed to get money to support a drug habit); or that it may illuminate the behavior of marijuana smokers but not of embezzlers.

This argument has been summarized succinctly by Milton Mankoff (1971):

> The failure of those whose work falls within the boundaries of the labeling tradition to develop typologies that indicate which particular kinds of social deviance can be most fruitfully understood by using the concepts of labeling theory is a serious shortcoming which prevents evaluating the significance of their research. While labeling theorists may think they are only applying the principles of the labeling perspective to one form of deviation, their incidental endorsements of generalizability to other forms of deviant behavior make the critic wary of "straw men" arguments when he attempts to project the implications of specific research for general theory. Those who write about deviance from the labeling perspective, whether they feel they are being general theorists or not, should welcome an attempt to consider the limits of their model for explaining career deviance.

Processing as a turning point. Adherents of labeling suggest that when persons are apprehended and processed and a negative tag is consequently placed upon them, this becomes a point in their career that catapults them into further and greater deviance. They are picked on, suspected, falsely arrested, arrested for actions that would be ignored in others, and generally regarded as antisocial. As true as this may be in some instances, it is contradicted by a body of literature in which the label and the identification of the transgressor may constitute what Harold Garfinkel (1956) termed a "degradation ceremony," or a moment of "hitting bottom" for someone who has been living a furtive and precarious life in deviant ways. It can "bring him to his senses," frighten him into seeing the bleakness of his future, and cause him to seek assistance. The label, Mankoff (1971) and others contend, does not necessarily lead to career deviance. In fact, deviant people can be induced to relinquish their rule-violating behavior by the labeling process. Referring to the famed Bank Wiring Room study, Bernard Thorsell and Lloyd Klemke (1972) note:

> In that study, labels applied by members of one's own work group were more effective in controlling deviation from group norms

than was labeling carried out by management representatives with respect to formal orders contradicting the group norms concerning daily output.

They conclude:

> When the deviant person has some commitment to and is, therefore, sensitive to the evaluation of the labeler, the effect of the labeling process appears more likely to be positive than negative.

Many rehabilitation programs for alcoholics and drug addicts adopt the approach of using the label as a way of getting people to think about changing their lives. Admitting that one is a "junkie"—including the use of this pejorative term—is often the first step toward rehabilitation in programs run by ex-addicts; and in Alcoholics Anonymous there is a major emphasis on stating repeatedly, "I am an alcoholic." On the other hand, Sagarin (1975) found that self-acceptance of a label may convince an individual that the label identifies what he "is" rather than what he "does" and hence may block his efforts to think in terms of change.

Thorsell and Klemke, however, cite the work of Mary Cameron (1964), who found that once the label of "shoplifter" was placed on the novice pilferer, this ended the designated activity. But they would not reject the concept of a label as a reinforcer or stimulus to greater deviance; rather, they would refine it by introducing such elements as the stages of the individual's immersion in the activity at the time he is apprehended, the secrecy and confidentiality of the label, the relationship of the deviant to the labeler, and the ease with which the designation can be removed. These and other modifications and exceptions might well make labeling theory more useful, not less so, in evaluating the anticipated effects of a given social reaction. Several such modifications could make labeling an effective though limited guide to policy, both for society as a whole and for the individual seeking to reduce tension and manage a difficult situation.

No doubt one can make a good case both for the original labeling perspective, that the placing of the tag pushes someone into greater or secondary deviance, and for the modified view, that the label helps people to remove themselves from deviant pathways. In short, apprehension and tagging do not invariably result in secondary deviation and aggravated conditions, although they no doubt do in some instances. Social scientists have yet to work out the conditions and the types of persons for whom the deviant label brings forth these diverse reactions.

Labeling generates underdog ideology. The adherents of labeling look upon the world from the vantage point of the deviant. They see the deviant not so much as one who has precipitated a reaction against himself but as one who has been victimized. Further, the victimization is not brought about by social institutions and lack of opportunities nor primarily by psychological forces at work in early childhood but overwhelmingly by a society that has rejected and condemned him. The sociologists "take the side" of the deviant and seek to show how he is misunderstood, wronged, and stereotyped. Their vision of the world of normals and deviants is narrowed by this approach, as they bend every effort to show the deviant in a light in which condemnation will be alleviated. Their research is motivated by liberal ideology, not by the objective search for truth. They base their assumptions on a belief that reforms in official treatment by agencies of control will end the stigmatizing and negative labeling; thus, according to the underdog ideology, the agencies of control, not the transgressors, are "the bad guys."

Labeling as a revival of extreme cultural relativism. In the effort to focus on moral entrepreneurs who arouse the community against some rule-breakers and to show that it is the reaction of the hostile society that creates deviance, labeling tends to deny the intrinsic evil in some human acts. Even retrospectively, a perspective that "evil is in the eyes of the beholder" would not support the view of slavery or genocide as inherently bad. To the labeler, if these acts were not seen as bad by the society in which they took place, to condemn them would be an improper imposition of one's own value judgments and morality. This is in contrast to the generally held modified ethical-relativist stand, in which one attempts to see what is ethnocentric about one's values and to distinguish the modes of behavior that are peculiar to the customs of an individual society from those that are inherently evil.

Labeling as a denial of the independence and responsibility of the actor. Although labeling may promote deviance, increase it, push people to more serious acts than might have occurred without the label, "the label does not create the behavior in the *first place*" (Akers, 1968). The problem is whether the label created the deviance, not the behavior that was so tagged. Here, labeling fails in all but a few instances, for it underemphasizes the role of the behavior in inciting the original societal denigration and reaction. In fact, labeling theorists emphasize various types of behavior in which the act itself caused no difficulty until crusaders took it upon themselves to arouse an apathetic or even an acquiescent public. Turning Durkheim upside down, they downplay the acts that brought forth the outrage and emphasize the outrage that created the deviant character of the behavior (although not, of course, the behavior itself).

Sometimes it appears that labeling theorists are ignoring the behavior that produces the negative societal reaction, as if to indicate that the reaction is either prior to the behavior or is haphazard and unpredictable. Surely there are some who are falsely accused and falsely suspected, but for the most part the acts do precede the reaction, provoke it, and create it, and in that sense the behavior is a proper avenue for study. However, deviance as an area of investigation for the student of human behavior must include both the act and the hostile reaction. The societal reaction is an integral part of the two-sided relationship, but it may be (and usually is) a response to the unacceptable behavior, not a production of "the differential treatment of persons by others."

Labeling ignores the problem of etiology. Labeling theorists often state that too much attention has been paid to etiology. For them, etiology is irrelevant; the main concern should be with how people are designated deviant by others, not with how people come to do certain things that earn them the label of deviant. If one starts from the concept that deviant is not inherent in the act or in the actor, it follows that it is wasteful to concern oneself with the factors that led to a person's becoming deviant. But from the viewpoint of the critics of labeling, this is not only a valuable area of social-scientific work but also one that might prevent many people from maturing into a life of difficulty and suffering. From the labeling perspective, they would not suffer if only they were not persecuted. Nevertheless, labeling could be reconciled with an interest in etiology and prevention; it just hasn't been done, except in rare instances. There is no reason one cannot focus both on the origins of drug addiction, for example, and on the amplification of deviance because of the societal reaction to the addict.

Labeling turns away from rehabilitation. Labeling not only generates little interest in etiology and prevention but also pays little attention to rehabilitation. The problem, the labelists say, is not to correct people who are disobeying rules but to stop stigmatizing and condemning them. The problem is not what activities on the part of the inmate led to institutionalization or how he can be changed, but what the institution does to dehumanize him. There is an inherent assumption that if only society were to cease oppressive stigmatization, people would be relatively happy in their formerly deviant (but now only offbeat, unusual, or nonconforming) roles.

This orientation is, of course, totally inapplicable to violent and predatory crime. Thomas Szasz (1970) would apply it to hard-core narcotics users; Erich Goode (1970) and many others to marijuana users, Edwin Schur (1965), Szasz (1970), and Martin Hoffman (1968), among several others, to homosexuality. All these perspectives ignore two important facets: (1) Do these types of behavior selectively attract people who already have difficulties and disturbances? (2) Would these behaviors gratify people if only the social stigma were lifted? Instead, two other very important problems are posed: (1) Should society be changed, rather than the individual who resists and rejects what Nicholas Kittrie (1971) terms "enforced therapy"? (2) Are there better ways of dealing with some, many, or all of these people than by criminalization, exclusion from normal social activities, confinement, and other punitive measures?

For some, rehabilitation suggests illness, and they see the label of illness (particularly mental illness) as having pejorative connotations. They ask: Is there not a better way of looking upon the behavior than as illness? To which critics reply that posing the question in this manner, with the implication that the answer is in the affirmative, makes rehabilitation and therapy (voluntary therapy, let it be added) more difficult.

Labeling leaves little room for secret deviance. Some formulations by adherents of the labeling orientation state specifically that one is not deviant unless one has been apprehended. Hence discovery becomes the act by which the deviant is created or manufactured. In his effort to answer the question, "Who is the criminal?" Paul Tappan (1947) takes the extreme view that only one who has been convicted by a recognized court of law is a criminal; the undetected criminal is a self-contradictory expression, although the undetected murderer presumably exists, a paradox that cannot easily be unraveled. Others would say that a person is not a "social deviant" without apprehension; that is, that he has not become deviant in social relations and social processes.

Yet, this does not appear to be a necessary part of labeling theory, for one can return to its bedrock: namely, that the social condemnation creates greater difficulties than the original deviation. If this is true, as it might well be for some types of deviants, then the secret deviant lives in fear of exposure, knowing that at any moment he can suffer reprisals at the hands of a condemning society and further feeling that he is an inauthentic person both because he is doing things that are "wrong" and because he is unable to acknowledge his secret. Labeling thus seems to have made a gross overstatement of the importance of the visibility of the behavior of the deviant. Sometimes this merely becomes a matter of definition: the secret deviant will not be included within the scope of those who are being studied in the category of deviants. Thus, Thomas Scheff (1966:33) writes:

> For the purpose of this discussion, . . . rule-breaking will refer to a class of acts, violations of social norms, and deviance to particular acts which have been publicly and officially labeled as norm violations.

The implication in this statement is that "deviants" would refer to the particular actors who have been publicly and officially labeled norm violators, but it is possible, although the matter was not stated in clear terms, that it could refer to people who performed acts labeled norm violations even if the performers had not been publicly and officially identified.

It is true that there is no official court to determine whether one is guilty of a deviant act unless the act is also criminal or the person is declared mentally incompetent; but the labelists to a large extent incorporate the concepts of apprehension and public identification as a major theme, for they fit in with the idea that social reaction is crucial in the development of permanent and aggravated deviance. Thus, in Lemert's (1951:51) initial statement of his position:

> In order for deviation to provoke a community reaction, it must have a minimum degree of visibility; that is, it must be apparent to others and be identified as deviation. A vast amount of sexual deviation in our society is clandestine and consequently escapes the public eye, which is to say that it has low visibility, a fact probably related to the puritanical background in our culture. This is not to say that no social influence is present, since the deviant in such cases may still, through the action of covert symbolic processes, imagine the reaction of "others" to his behavior and acquire feelings of guilt or anxiety. However, he or she does avoid the traumatic impact of public identification as an immoral person and also evades the sequence of differential reactions and penalty which follows such an identification.

In the subsequent literature, there has been considerable confusion between identification of a type of behavior as negative and identification of an individual as one who indulges in such behavior. Thus, in his study of societal reaction to homosexuality, Kitsuse (1962) describes how people came to suspect that others were interested in homosexual activities, but this is confounded with placing a negative label of deviant on all those so indulging or so motivated. Becker writes of the deviant as one to whom the label has been successfully applied. If this means only the apprehended individual, it omits a large number of important persons, and sometimes Becker and his colleagues seem to so indicate. If it is meant to include classes of persons to whom the label has been applied, it is true, but it becomes almost tautological.

Labeling focuses on official reaction, whereas a great deal of social stigma is unofficial. By "societal reaction to deviance," most labeling adherents have referred primarily to official processing by agencies with power, if not governmental bodies, then quasigovernmental. They appear to have downplayed informal control, or what might be identified as social reaction in contrast to societal.

But ridicule, as noted, can be a tremendous force, making the deviant feel ashamed, aggravating his feeling of unworthiness. While this is in no way incompatible with labeling, the latter approach has led to a one-sided view because of the significance given to the placing of the label.

The Label as a Clarifier

Sometimes the "societal reaction" sociologists seem to be arguing that it is the tag itself, and the hostile reaction that accompanies it, that can bring forth deviant behavior. It is possible, however, that the label can identify a person's behavior to himself, clarifying it in a manner that permits greater freedom of choice and consequently freedom to decide whether to change.

Psychiatrist E. Fuller Torrey (1973:17) writes: "The naming process, the use of words as symbols for what is wrong, is effective not because of the knowledge per se that the words convey," and then, quoting Claude Lévi-Strauss, "but because this knowledge makes possible a specific experience, in the course of which conflicts materialize in an order and on a level permitting their free development and leading to their resolution." Although Torrey here is referring to mental illness and the therapeutic process, it can be seen that placing a label on a person or type of behavior need not lead to aggravation of a situation, as adherents of the labeling perspective have contended.

Labeling: A Much-Needed Corrective

Nevertheless, it is true that in some instances the social hostility amplifies and aggravates the deviance; that people become paranoid because they are looked upon and treated with suspicion; that mental illness may be aggravated, may in fact become mental illness, because mild eccentric behavior is labeled "lunacy"; and so one could continue. Labeling has made sociologists aware that social hostility sometimes has an effect opposite that intended or desired. It is a perspective on nonnormative behavior that has many errors and pitfalls but that cannot be ignored in the development of sociological theory or social policy. Labeling may make deviance more difficult to carry out or easier to justify. In any event, the performer of deviant acts has many things to consider, as has the sociologist.

6

Coping with Deviance

The Burdens of Secrecy

How does the norm violator cope with the problems of the world around him? This matter was little studied by sociologists until the work of Erving Goffman (1963); note particularly the subtitle of his work on this subject: *Stigma: Notes on the Management of Spoiled Identity.*

An individual who has been designated or thinks of himself as a transgressor may be self-righteous, as is the political deviant, certain that his is the correct path and that those who condemn him are wrong, if not evil. Or he may conceal his activities. However, under most conditions (the spy would be an exception), secrecy requires an enormous expenditure of energy for ego strength and self-justification. If secrecy is adopted as a strategy, it would suggest either shame or fear of punishment.

Although many deviants are unknown to the public, at least in that aspect of their selves that would define them negatively, this is not universally the case. In many instances, the nature of the status or acts is such that it is highly visible and hence beyond the possibility of concealment. In other instances, it is almost never made public. Between these two poles there are many gradations and variations.

Several conditions may bring about an "unmasking" of the deviant. This may occur merely by apprehension. Predatory crime is committed by secret deviants, who want their identity to remain unknown and who take measures to prevent themselves from being seen by any but the victims—and not always by the victims. In the case of burglary, the act may be planned for a time when the victims are away; in rape, truck hijacking, and kidnapping, the victims may be blindfolded, so that they never see the offenders. In these cases, it is the act of being apprehended that creates the visibility of the individual—that is, identifies him with the crime.

These situations are closely related to another category, in which the act is taken for granted and accepted as an ordinary event until it becomes public knowledge. At that point, and by virtue of that fact, it becomes deviant, unlike violent crime, which is deviant even when the perpetrator's identity is unknown. Examples include influence peddling, fee splitting, and the signing of restrictive racial covenants. A disbarred lawyer says, "I did what practically every lawyer does, but somebody made a fuss about it." Getting caught was not the crime, but it did transform the act into a deviant one, through exposure and visibility. This type of transformation takes place through what might be called deprivatization, a most dramatic example of which was the accidental discovery of the White House tapes.

There have even been legal codifications that grant recognition to an act, permitting it if it is kept circumspect and prohibiting it if it is made public. There are, for instance, local statutes prohibiting open cohabitation of unmarried persons where such behavior flouts the morality of the community. The wording of the laws as well as the interpretations of the courts have given evidence that sanctions are not meant to be applied against those who engage in nonmarital sexual activity (including the sharing of a dwelling) in an unobtrusive manner.

Instances of this sort, in which those on the borderline between the normative and the deviant slip into the latter category, may be considered examples of "going public." The act or status was previously existent, but it was its deprivatization that constituted the crucial condition for being labeled deviant.

Going public may also be a voluntary act, in which one's attitudes or behavior would be ignored if it was not blatantly advertised. In American society, for example, few seem to care if one is an atheist. It is considered a person's own business, an entirely private matter, but something that one is not supposed to proclaim publicly. As has been said in the popular folklore of sexual relations: "All right, but you don't do it in Macy's window," and only if you do it in Macy's window is it considered offensive. This might be called the creation of deviance through self-advertisement.

Visibility may result from a deliberate effort by the individual to cope with a problem or to advance an idea and proselytize for it. In the former category, one may place the theme, so popular among some people engaged in homosexual activities, of "coming out." By ceasing to conceal their activities and propensities, they feel better able to lobby, to advance their organizational struggles, to propagandize for their way of looking at their own activities and at themselves, to counteract shame, and to disarm the hostile world. By contrast, the political deviant (unless he wishes to use the tactics of a spy) goes public because it is the only road open to advance the policies to which he is committed.

The deliberate attempt to achieve visibility is a strategy not open to all types of deviants. It requires one or several of the following conditions: (1) an ideology that supports one's own self-righteousness and the propriety of one's activities; (2) the feeling that the condition is immutable or that one will not relinquish one's ideas; (3) frustration that one attributes to concealment of the deviance; (4) the belief that one is relatively immune, for whatever reason, from greater stigmatization as a result of going public; and (5) a feeling of collective strength in a portion of the deviant population to which one looks for support.

Whether visibility is inevitable (as in the case of the obese) or deliberately chosen (as in the case of the militant atheist), the visible deviant has options that are not open to the secret deviant. The visible deviant is both more and less vulnerable, in that he probably lives in a world of greater discrimination but lesser fear than the secret deviant.

Then there is the problem of the false accusation—an imputation of deviance that comes about through the search for the perpetrator of a disvalued act reported to have taken place, or it may be that there never was such an act, and the accusation is false insofar as both the event and the accused are concerned. False accusations may result from and in rumor and gossip or official proceedings and prosecution. Criminal proceedings by their very nature impute deviance, but this remains only an imputation so long as there is no verdict of guilty. Until adjudicated guilty, an accused is said to be innocent, and this is indicated by the mandatory use of the word "alleged," without which a newspaper libels a defendant. But the strength of the imputation is expressed in the saying, "Where there's smoke, there's fire." However, one may be guilty of having dissenting beliefs, and then, as in the Rosenberg "atom spy" trial, conclusions about espionage are drawn, buttressed by little other than those beliefs.

Sexual behavior often gives rise to suspicions of deviance. False accusations can result from jealousy or may be deliberately created in order to justify disruption of an agonizing relationship.

Suspicion need not be and often is not articulated. A state of tense equilibrium grows up, in which A suspects B of having performed a deviant act, B suspects A of suspecting B, and A suspects B of suspecting A of suspecting B, almost *ad infinitum.*

It is the fate of the suspected deviant that he can almost never be found innocent. There is no court of law, only the court of public opinion, and its verdict depends on whims and fancies. Protestations of innocence may serve only to draw attention to the rumor or charge, very much as do the shouts and protests of an entirely sane man who is taken away in a straitjacket.

Coping with Secrecy

Many secret deviants develop a circle of friends and colleagues who are "in the know" while intermingling with others who are not. In other cases the secret is so closely kept that no one but the deviant himself knows. Impotence is an example of an extremely stigmatizing condition that is hardly ever mentioned except to a physician or therapist and may be unknown except to the man himself and his sexual partner. Impotence does not lead to interaction with others sharing the same problem, except in the limited case of group therapy, and then only if the therapist structures his groups by bringing together those whose problems are similar.

The question of who should be in the know and who should not is a major one for the secret deviant. A married man and a married woman are having an affair, unbeknown to their respective spouses and children, but they may have a circle of office friends, motel owners, and others who do know. For the secret deviants, the in-the-know circle provides a milieu for "letting their hair down," a situation in which the fear that the mask will be penetrated is put aside. However, this is not an inevitable aspect of being in the presence of those in the know. Sometimes there is a tacit understanding that a given situation is unmentionable even though each person present is knowledgeable about the other.

The secret deviant often exaggerates the disaster that will befall him if his discrediting characteristic becomes known. Whether his fear is justified depends both on the nature of that characteristic and on the social, educational, and other statuses of the vulnerable person. The revelation of a highly discrediting characteristic is often greeted by indifference. "So what?" people say. Before he goes public, the secret deviant calculates whether most of his friends and acquaintances will have that reaction or make some other gesture expressing lack of indignation, even if he is unaware of the attention he is paying to the problem. Is it in the nature of the condition and of the social atmosphere that his deprivatization will bring sympathy and pity, or only condemnation? To what extent is he morally responsible for his deviance? Does his unmasking make him threatening to others? Furthermore, what are his other statuses? Are they sufficient to override the denigrated one? If he is disclosing something in his past, has he been rehabilitated? Suppose that a man harbors a fear that some day it will be learned that he escaped from prison some twenty years earlier, and suppose that he has been married and regularly employed since that time; such a man will often find friends and neighbors rallying to his side after his secret is exposed. "It's a great burden off my mind to have this come out after all these years," he will say.

Sometimes the deviance consists in the very fact that it is secret. A person with one set of characteristics who pretends to have another, where neither identity is necessarily deviant in itself, is called an impostor. In race relations, this exists when a light-skinned black person pretends to be white, and it is spoken of as "passing." The word might well be used to cover any such deliberately false claim, where the deviance resides only in the deception, as, for instance, one who passes as a physician without having the credentials. To pass means to be successful in navigating with the assumed identity.

A special case of passing would be transvestism, for it is clear that there is nothing deviant about being male or being female, or about appearing in male or in female attire. The socially disapproved act resides only in the pretense. When a male successfully wears the mask, one may say that he is passing as a female. Male transvestites speak of themselves when in feminine attire as being "dressed," but this, unlike passing, does not imply any degree of success in deluding an onlooker not in the know. Although the word "dressed" is derived from the fact that one puts on certain apparel, it could be extended to the idea of wearing a mask or a costume, even in a figurative sense, and would be useful to indicate situations in which a performer can pick up the mask and then lay it aside.

Transvestism has also supplied a term to describe the state when passing is unsuccessful and people suspect or know that a mask is being worn. The transvestites say that they are being "read," or that others can "read" them. To read means to understand that an identity is assumed. It would be a valuable term for general use in the study of deviance because it deals with the way secret deviants are able to communicate without others knowing about it, and how some others do see through the disguise, sometimes without revealing that they see through it. What results, in short, is a conspiracy of pretense.

The problem of passing becomes very complex when there are psychological motivations, so that gratification is increased if others know how successful the mask actually is. This makes for a self-contradictory situation: one wants to pass, but wants others to know that one is passing. The knowledge must not be derived from being read, because then the costume is a failure. Transvestites sometimes handle this by having exclusive parties. One such party was observed by a trained therapist who was an accepted outsider, Hugo Beigel (1969). According to Beigel, everyone knew who was in costume, and the greatest compliment the transvestites could receive was to be told, "I'd never know, nobody could ever tell."

An aspect of secret deviance is the skeleton-in-the-closet syndrome. This often involves what Goffman (1963) calls "courtesy stigma," or what might be termed "stigma fallout," similar to what is popularly known as guilt by association. It is a matter of being discredited because a family member or some other close associate has the negative characteristic. Having a mentally retarded child in the family was often kept a deep secret, perhaps, some have suggested, because of the imputation of genetic defect in the parents and hence in all other family members, with concomitant reduction of the marriageability of brothers and sisters. Whatever modicum of rationality there may be in this explanation for concealment of mental retardation, it is very difficult to use to account for the stigma when a family member has an illegitimate child, is sexually promiscuous or homosexual, goes to prison, or enters into an interracial marriage. Deviance, even when it is a matter of birth, accident, or other blamelessness, is seen as a moral blight, and to the extent that one is associated with it, one is contaminated.

In managing a courtesy stigma, the characteristic is not contagious, but the disvaluation it carries with it most definitely is. Secrecy is one of the available mechanisms for handling this problem, because the deviant can sometimes be hidden, as in another city, in an institution, literally in a barn or attic, or, much less literally, in a closet. Secrecy, however, is not the only option used in the case of courtesy stigma, and it is being resorted to less frequently, it would appear, when the stigma derives from a biological condition and even for behavioral problems. Students have told us of acute alcoholism in their families (usually a father, sometimes a brother, occasionally a mother). They do not hide the fact from their friends but overcome the stigma by meeting it head-on. In calling for sympathy, they forestall rejection.

One strategy for concealing deviance may involve engaging in another form of deviance, also secret, but the second deliberately assumed to protect oneself from the damaging results if the first should become known. An example is the flat-chested woman who wears falsies. When she is scorned for wearing falsies, she is doubly scorned, both for the imposture and for the anatomical deficiency that motivated her to try it. In one of Goffman's works (1969:19–21), the assumption of a second deviance to conceal a first is called a counter-uncovering move, as distinct from the ordinary mask or cover.

Kitsuse (1962) studied the process by which normals become suspicious of others, and hence transform the secret deviant into the imputed one. Among other things, he found that the normals would retrospectively reinterpret the behavior of the secret deviant after an incident had occurred or after they had heard a rumor that led them to suspect homosexuality. In certain respects, however, there is a wide difference between how one finds out about homosexuals and about certain other types of people with secrets. Homosexuals are motivated both toward secrecy (or at least they were until recently) and toward revelation because it is sexually advantageous to reveal oneself, so long as it is to people within a carefully controlled group. Some of Kitsuse's subjects were propositioned—the coach started to rub the boy's back, the man in the taxi put his hand on the other fellow's knee. A revelation of this type, however, is not the same as going public, although it can have the same eventual consequences.

Like homosexuals, call girls have to be known about, within a limited circle, in order to obtain clients; addicts, in order to make the connection; the mentally ill in order to receive treatment. However, many people who seek help also attempt to conceal from others the nature of the help they are getting. Alcoholics who enter treatment sometimes tell their friends they are recovering from emotional exhaustion or severe physical illness. Prior to legalized abortion, some women took "vacations" in Puerto Rico in order to end their unwanted pregnancies. In these instances, someone has to know, but he does not necessarily have to have full information. On the other hand, in many other types of deviance, not only is there no advantage in self-revelation (except possibly catharsis), but there is seldom rumor unless it is specifically planted or well-founded. People do not go around "wondering if he's one" when the "one" refers to an ex-convict or rapist, a child molester or the brother of a mongoloid, to the extent they do homosexuals or, on occasion, former mental patients. If they wonder whether someone is a mugger or a confidence man, this is a matter of self-protective fear or suspicion of large segments of the population, not specific to a given individual.

When the secret deviant is strongly motivated toward revelation about himself, he may, rather than go public, confide in a small group or even one person. Before he removes his mask, he sizes up the other or others and decides that the next step can be taken with safety. The cues, verbal and nonverbal, are arranged in an escalating order. Each leads to the next, and each suggests or discloses more than the previous. However, an avenue of retreat must be left open so that the discarded mask can be retrieved if it should become necessary to do so. One can say that the secret deviant does not burn his bridges behind him; more accurately, he abandons these bridges, always aware of alternate roads, bridges, and tunnels. There is an avenue of escape, consisting in recovery of the mask, with sufficient aplomb so that one can pretend both that it is not a mask and that one has never discarded it.

The Twain That Must Not Meet

If getting through the day is, as Goffman has it, a matter of impression management for everyone, it is the more so for the deviant, and doubly so for the secret deviant, the invisible deviant, the pretended deviant, the falsely accused, and the impostor. If all men wear masks and deliberately strive to present impressions of themselves, deviants do so with greater awareness of the incongruence between different levels of reality, and often with guilt and shame. Unless excellent self-justifications can be constructed, one tends to internalize the attitudes of the culture toward oneself. If one lives a lie, one's life is fraught with fear and with tremendous risk, for his house of cards may collapse at any time.

But the pretended and the secret deviants are involved with a self-conscious presentation of the self. Since they cannot be their "natural selves," since this would endanger the interaction they so precariously maintain, they must decide what that unnatural self is like in order to make it convincing. This may lead them into a study of others, even into rehearsal of the roles they are going to play. For a person to pretend to be what he believes he is not means that he must have a mental image of how the staged self should be presented. In his dramatic presentation, he has no director to guide and correct his every move. More fearful that he will underplay the part than overplay it, he often manifests overreaction, and sometimes selects an atypical stereotype as a model to imitate. The police informer tries to be the perfect hippie or radical or Klansman; the transvestite often shows exaggerated traits that are not feminine but, rather, effeminate.

There is a dynamic interaction between the worlds of visibility and invisibility. A man may travel from the latter to the former —the coming-out process. But he may also go in the opposite direction, the going-into-hiding process. A former convict or mental patient carefully conceals his past status and in so doing conceals his present one. This may require some manipulation, sometimes a change of locale or of significant persons with whom he interacts, and even a change of name. Extreme cases of such rebuilding of the past can be seen in people who have undergone a transsexual operation. Some postoperative cases present themselves as just that: former males, now females. But others conceal the past and ask for change on birth certificates, school records, and elsewhere. Adoptive parents are sometimes able to get birth records to list them as the natural parents, or if this is impossible, to list the natural parents as unknown.

How one chooses the people who are to know about one's secret, how and why one excludes all others, and, most important, how one keeps from confusing cues so that the twain do not meet are little studied aspects of secrecy. The process takes a great toll on the secret deviant, and it is one of the arguments made by those who call on homosexuals to come "out of the closet." There are, however, disadvantages in "deviance avowal," to use the expression of Ralph Turner (1972). The greatest drawback is that it often acts as a reinforcement or fixation of the deviant status and closes the door on change or development that might otherwise have been pursued.

In any case, secrecy is a burden, accompanied by fear, by a constant and conscious search for disidentifiers. It often reduces a feeling of self-worth, and it gives rise to anger, both against

others and against oneself. It is a high price to pay for violating
the norms of one's society. Following the lonesome road, a strategy of secrecy, involves paying certain tolls, while being overt
about one's deviance often involves joining with others and paying dues!

DEVIANTS AMONG THEIR OWN

One strategy open to deviants, as it is to all those who differ
from many of the people surrounding them, is to form a group
of people with life styles like their own, or, if such a group already
exists, to become part of it. That certain types and kinds of
deviants tend to congregate together is quite apparent, a fact that
has at times brought forth expressions of public indignation.
Under some conditions, the intermingling and interaction are
limited to the portion of their lives that involves their disvalued
trait; under other circumstances, they derive their deviance from
the fact that they have mingled together; and finally, there are
conditions in which they tend to develop large portions of their
lives in close interaction with others similarly situated. A variety
of patterns emerges; they take on different forms, with some
gains apparently to be extracted from the existence of what might
be termed "a life-style group," and perhaps some potential losses
as well.

Considerable controversy has centered on the question of
whether these groups constitute actual subcultures of deviants.
Some of the debate involves the rather complex matter of the
definition of a subculture. It may be identified as a group of
people partially but never entirely removed from a larger society
of which they are a part, who interact among themselves to a
large extent and in important sectors of their lives, sharing some
common values and outlooks on the world that impart a sense of
ingroup solidarity not extended to others. Milton Yinger (1960)
had made an important differentiation between the subculture
and the counterculture, before Theodore Roszak (1969) and others popularized the latter term as synonymous with the life style
of youth in rebellion against the overtechnologized society. For

Yinger, what characterizes the counterculture is that its values and activities are in direct conflict with those of the larger society, so that the two cannot peacefully coexist with mutual toleration.

To illustrate, a small religious group might constitute a subculture. However, if it should proselytize in a manner that creates hostility to any ecumenical spirit, and if it suggests to its adherents lines of action that would be beyond the limits of tolerance of society (such as polygamy), then it would move into the realm of the counterculture. Some political deviants might well be in conflict, most directly and even violently, with the surrounding institutions, yet contact among adherents could be so infrequent, albeit meaningful, that they would hardly be a subculture, much less a counterculture. Here, one would speak of a social movement in conflict with the power structures of the society.

In addition to the concepts of subculture and counterculture, a third pattern emerges, the alternate culture, which might more accurately be considered an alternate life style. However, not all types of deviants develop close and frequent interrelationships with similarly situated people. Some by their nature are loners. Even when they work in groups of twos and threes, they are not in contact and do not share a common outlook with other individuals and groups. There are no groups of child molesters, for example, or of rapists. This is not to deny that there could be frequent interaction among violence-prone males, that such a group, among other things, might include more than its share of men who commit rape; or among sexual freedomists who, as part of their program, would approve of child molestation by adults and attract to their ranks some persons who are interested in or involved with children in an overtly sexual manner. In general, however, these people act and behave as individuals, and if they share with others a certain stigma, fear, knowledge of how to commit their acts, and other traits, there is nevertheless insufficient interaction and value-sharing among them for one to speak of their being immersed in a life style, no less a subculture.

At the other extreme, there are those whose deviance derives exclusively from the fact that they interact with others like themselves—for example, a group of young people who form a commune, obtain some real estate, live off the land, and have a distinctive life style clearly unlike that of their neighbors, with whom their relationships are minimal. If this were a unique group of a dozen or a score of people, its total influence on a society of two hundred million would be so slight that the matter might be ignored except by their families and neighbors. These communards, however, do not restrict their relationships to those with whom they cohabit but develop a sense of identification with groups of like nature throughout the nation, influencing them and being influenced, and with some ease in exchanging members from time to time. The simultaneous development of many such groups, the commonality of their ideology and way of life, their demarcation from those unlike themselves, all impart to them some of the traits of an alternate way of life. To the extent that they constitute no viable threat to those who are not part of their groups but are a beacon to the disaffected, they can probably be conceptualized most lucidly as an alternate culture.

Inasmuch as life-style groups do emerge among some deviants but not among others, sociologists are concerned with the conditions conducive to such development. The major one would be that the nature of the trait differentiating such people from others requires goods, services, or other desiderata best fulfilled by the creation of a network of similarly situated men and women, or even others unlike them but willing and eager to serve them. Further, the vulnerability of the deviant to the sanctions of society should not be seriously increased by such interaction and the ensuing enhanced visibility.

Of the first criterion, one might contrast such groups as drug-users, winos, abortion seekers (before the liberalization of the laws in many jurisdictions of the United States), prostitutes, homosexuals, check forgers, and partisans of the antiwar movement of the late 1960s and early 1970s. Each becomes or became involved to a different extent, in a different way, and to bring about different goals, in a way of life that deviated from the norms of the mainstream of American society.

The drug-users, limiting this term to users of hard-core and completely illegal narcotics, would be a prime example of people who are compelled to develop and use a subterranean network as a strategy for survival. Heroin-users generally, perhaps physicians and nurses excepted, need contacts. They must have a connection to obtain a fix, and they generally need several such connections, because one may not be available at the right time and place. Their lives become increasingly embroiled in a succession of acts centered around the drug scene and around others involved in it; enjoying the high, letting it wear off, scheming to get money to enjoy the next, borrowing and lending and even stealing within the charmed circle, locating the connection, avoiding arrest, pushing and dealing, and then getting through the day until it is time to repeat these performances. Or, at some point, getting cleaned, permanently or temporarily, exchanging experiences about cold turkey with denizens of their world, resolving to relinquish the drug life, becoming part of a program that is still drug-oriented although not in the same sense that the earlier period of life had been, and, finally, rehabilitating completely or splitting to start the cycle again, but this time with a cheaper habit, at least to begin with.

All of these acts require knowledge of others like oneself, knowing whom to trust, how to proceed. Two simultaneous occurrences complement each other: growing dependence on other users and rejection of and by the square world. There is an increasing inability to function with family, friends, and acquaintances who are not part of a drug-using community. Language, outlook, commonality of interests, mutual dependence, significant knowledge, and survival techniques—all bring the apprentice addict into closer and more frequent relationships both with other apprentices and with veterans of their war with the authorities. Even for those who leave their addict relationships and return to their families to sleep and eat, perhaps to beg or steal, or for those who take brief leaves from their companions for work or school, involvement with the addict world grows, entwining and ensnaring the addict until it encompasses a near-totality of life.

The addict groups, like those many others involving deviants, do not add up to a single cohesive and unified collectivity, in the sense that small ethnic groups like the Basques in America or religious sects like snake cultists usually become. An addict lifestyle group is more amorphous and poorly defined, with members who drift in and out. It consists of a large number of little collections of persons, quick to learn of the other islands in the same or other cities. They are islands that those in the know can easily locate and that may differ from one another in important respects, such as racial composition, degree of poverty, types of illegal activities other than commerce in drugs. However, their common characteristics and their isolation from the mainstream of society are sufficient to conceptualize these people as denizens of a deviant submerged and alternate world. They had been brought together primarily by the need for an illegal service, but they found in one another mutual understanding, acceptance, and reinforcement; they found others like themselves with whom they could make contact, who would grasp the nature of their troubles even if they could offer nothing more than empty solace. Without some subcultural network, illegal trafficking in drugs would be extremely difficult.

This is not true of winos or check forgers. The latter, in fact, are on safer grounds if they work alone or with only one other person. They do not need an apprenticeship, although here and there the forger may pick up a few pieces of useful instruction. In short, the forger is a loner for two reasons: there is no need to be otherwise, and there would be disadvantages rather than gain from interacting with other forgers. Fraternization with people like himself would only attract attention and might result in arrest, in addition to offering unwanted competition by saturating a single area (as a bank, store, or town) with more bad checks than it can assimilate.

Nor does one require similar deviants to get the bottle of cheap wine, the can of beer, or the low-grade whisky that single-room-only habitués, derelicts, and Skid Row inhabitants imbibe. Yet, unlike respectable alcoholics of all social classes, these people do drift together with people like themselves, impelled not by a need to be part of a network of illegal sales but by the quest for social acceptance and relief from rejection and loneliness.

On the one hand, the groupings of deviants offer the rejected person ego reinforcement; on the other, they tend to imprison him in the unacceptable way of life. To the extent that relationships with other deviants fill the hours of his day and his needs, they not only will be fulfilling but will also encourage his further withdrawal from the world of normals. A person who has been rejected, or has felt rejected, by ordinary people at every turn, who has been or felt insulted and wounded on innumerable occasions—such an individual may well see withdrawal as a step toward liberation. But it is at the same time a step that the world of normals would call backward, separating people from the society around them by a greater chasm than was caused by the original deviant act or the hostile reaction to it.

Membership in the deviant groupings often produces a sense of pride. Mutual reinforcement leads to the evolution of a shared world view, in which persons lead others and themselves to an outlook on reality they come more and more to assimilate as the only true reality. Rather than having role models who have "rehabilitated" or "reformed," they look to those who have tried this road and failed, and they come to believe that if they try they too will fail. At the same time, they believe that the effort is not worth it, even if it is successful, for their own life is a good and worthwhile one. Among some similarly situated persons there may indeed be a great dramaturgical put-on to build solidarity, as David Matza (1964) suggests about juveniles: none believes in the delinquent values, but each must make the pretense to all the others. It is as if each individual believes in the values of family, school, and society in general, but such belief systems have lost their respectability among the defiant and often rebellious youths. But the question remains: Do the youths eventually come to accept the values that originally they only pretended to espouse?

In a life-style group, people learn not only values but cues from one another as well. Transsexuals, for example, must learn how to give the right answers to psychiatrists and other doctors so as to appear in the light most likely to convince these authorities to endorse their operation. This is not unlike the learning experience that takes place in prison, where people are coached on the types of answers to give to social workers, parole officers, and others.

Some deviant groups retain an amorphous character. The nature of their deviance and of the social situation may require that they be hidden from public light as much as possible. Those who move in and out of networks of black marketeers or smuggling rings would prefer that the very existence of this maze of relationships be unknown except to the select ingroup. Other social deviants wish to influence public policy in regard either to themselves or to the world. If there is sufficient oppression to make their condition intolerable but sufficient democratic tolerance to make their protest possible, they can emerge into social movements and highly organized groups. The development of a social movement, however, should not be seen as a displacement of the more amorphous groups; it is, rather, a part of it, one in which usually only a small part of the eligible population participates. This fraction might be called "a vanguard," but this is an emotionally loaded term suggesting that it is leading the masses. Such may well be the case, but the contrary may be true: the masses (that is, of deviants or eligibles) may be hostile, indifferent, or unaware.

Even when alternate life-style groups are thriving, not all those who make the deviant identification become part of them. A prostitute can be a loner or a frequent commingler with a world of prostitutes and pimps, and the same is true of those involved in homosexuality, drug addiction, or alcoholism, but each to a different extent and with unlike consequences. Sociology will find a fruitful field of study in contrasting those who navigate among deviants like themselves with others who share the discredited or discreditable trait but remain aloof. What determines the pathway for each individual? And with what results? What happens when the once anonymous and powerless loners organize for the purpose of developing political activity? It appears that the expressed need to be somebody and to be recognized as a member of a group is at this point being voiced by the most despised and disvalued.

PROTEST AND THE STRUGGLE TO CHANGE SOCIETY

Those who transgress, violate norms, and become (or are considered) deviant may seek to change their ways. With what success depends in part on the nature and type of deviance. Some renounce their former ways because they have been convinced that they were wrong; these would include, for example, the members of disapproved religious or political movements. Others find refuge in psychotherapy, or find new opportunities that replace the old, or are discouraged by their former activities and by the punishments they have suffered.

One way of coping with deviance, then, is to renounce it and, as a reformed sinner, seek to be welcomed into society. But rehabilitation is an individual solution that solves the problem by shifting the individual from the ranks of the condemned to those of the embraced. Conversely, one might attempt to reduce or eliminate certain forms of deviance by changing society. Instead of working to bring the strayed individual back into the world of respectability, one works toward changing that world, either to conform with the ways of the deviant or to broaden its limits of tolerance so as to accept paths that were formerly condemned. That society does undergo change can be seen in its attitude toward divorce, abortion, interracial marriage, explicit presentation of sex in literature and the mass media, premarital cohabitation, and homosexuality. Advocates of interracial integration, a group once deviant, have seen their position become the dominant (at least the official) ideology of American life.

Not all forms of deviance lend themselves to acceptance through change in the social mores. Most people who disobey norms accept that what they are doing is wrong and find it unthinkable that the society might accept their ways as the right ones. This is particularly true of nonnormative actions that are criminal, especially felonies. Rape, burglary, robbery, and even some minor shoplifting cannot be accepted into the ways of society as good and proper, although in individual cases there might be mitigating circumstances that would reduce the extent of culpability.

Nevertheless, for prohibited or condemned sexual acts between consenting partners, for the use of many now prohibited or regulated drugs, and for such activities as gambling, prostitution, and pimping, many persons see no reason for legal or social condemnation. This would contrast with the mother who has brutally beaten a child who lied to her or a man who has murdered his wife's lover. These people are not concerned with changing laws or mores; they probably had no thought that what they were doing was in any way wrong, or that they had no moral right to perform the act.

The struggle to change social mores has sometimes centered around the question of law. The process by which a previously condemned act is removed from the penal codes, and thus becomes legal, is known as "decriminalization." It is useful in discussing decriminalization to distinguish between acts that are considered by large portions of the populace to be perfectly proper (gambling, for example, or in recent years abortion) and acts that are deplored but that some people feel should be handled outside the law or by regulation rather than by illegalization (drug addiction or prostitution, for example).

There are limits to the number and types of deviant acts that can be accepted or deviant people who can be looked on without stigma. Theft, rape, and homicide are definitely outside the limits of tolerance of a society. It is true that a society often tolerates theft from the poor by corporate entities, theft of an election by powerful political bosses, but without suggesting that such acts should be condoned or that they are less antisocial than shoplifting or pickpocketing, the fact remains that some types of theft and other illegal acts cannot be accepted. Even those described above as being condoned are at least officially condemned by lawmakers and other cultural leaders.

Other norms, however, can be challenged and their legitimacy attacked. Thus it was with the great civil rights movement of the sixties and with various norms of sexual behavior. The old ways can be and have been challenged by single voices of protest, sometimes powerful voices of people highly placed, or the challenge may be launched by and bring into its train large numbers of affected deviants. There is a shift from denial, escape, and concealment to the often angry voices of social protest.

A sense of self-righteousness is an aid in the development of a protest movement, but the reverse is also true, for the movement itself brings forth a sense of the dignity and propriety of what one is doing. Social-protest movements assist in breaking through the secrecy that has so often enshrouded the lives of deviants, lifting their fear of discovery by openly proclaiming their identity. They are also likely to divert attention and energy away from rehabilitation by providing scientific, political, and general ideological arguments in favor of the current form of life. This has certainly been one of the effects of the homosexual protest. On the other hand, the protests, less organized and articulate but most important, on the part of prisoners, ex-convicts, and ex-mental patients offer this same sense of dignity, but without deflecting attention from personal change.

While more tolerant attitudes in society have been accompanied by the "treatment" approach to deviance, as opposed to the "punishment" orientation, many of those involved in social-protest movements have rejected the implication that they are "sick" or in need of treatment. Persons involved in the homophile movement, for example, do not wish to be rehabilitated but demand that any redefinition of their behavior be in the direction of regarding it as a variant of "normal" behavior. In the past, many organizations of deviants have urged the use of softer labels for their members, in effect admitting their differentness in order to attain a modicum of acceptance. Contemporary voluntary associations of deviant people, following the models of expression among oppressed ethnic minorities in American society, have attempted to redefine their differentness into desirable traits and have demanded recognition as well as acceptance of their social identities. The interplay between the need to be somebody, the available models of expression, and the organizational forms for protest is examined in the next section.

ORGANIZATIONS FOR CHANGING SOCIETY AND ONESELF

Social change is often brought about through protest, usually led by organized groups of people clearly identifying with an issue. America in recent years has seen various organizations in the feminist movement, formal groups struggling for and against the right to have abortions, people lobbying, marching, and boycotting on behalf of ethnic minorities. And there have been other protest organizations, including alcoholics, homosexuals, drug addicts, ex-prisoners, transvestites, and many others.

Most voluntary associations of deviants attempt to deal with the society's reaction to deviant behavior. There are essentially two types of organizations (or voluntary associations) of deviant people, characterized by divergent goals. One type is involved in an effort to change power relationships in the society, that is, to change social attitudes toward the deviants themselves. A second type, while also interested in alleviating social hostility, seeks primarily to change, reform, control, or rehabilitate the transgressor. Following individual adaptations, the escape from stigma takes on two divergent and usually mutually exclusive patterns, although there may be some convergence: (1) The deviant may escape from stigma by conforming to the norms of the society; that is, by "reforming," by relinquishing the stigmatizing behavior, a goal that has received widespread publicity under the rubrics of "corrections" and "rehabilitation"; or (2) he may escape from stigma by reforming the norms of society, by reducing the sanctions against his behavior; that is, by changing, not himself, but the rule-making others. In this case, he is obtaining from society a relinquishment of the stigmatization of his behavior. These two patterns may well constitute the most important single factor differentiating some of these associations from others.

Whether the goal of the deviant organization is to assist individuals in achieving more normative behavior or to change the attitudes of a hostile society, difficulties and contradictions manifest themselves. The act of joining may increase the stigma for the individual by transforming him from an invisible to a visible member of the socially disapproved category. But organizations meet this problem in two ways: by using anonymity to protect the individual, and by using association among those similarly situated as a mechanism for the reduction of social disvaluation.

With this conceptualization, one might foresee that groups in which individuals seek to change themselves would gain wide social approval from the greater society, except from those who are geographically and in other ways so close to the deviants that the congregation of individuals in an organization becomes threatening. Furthermore, these groups would function very much like group therapy; would often turn to religious or pseudoreligious concepts for reinforcement; would embrace many middle-class aims in an attempt to return to a life of propriety, while scoffing at the hypocrisy of the middle class that rejects and opposes them. Such a group would paint the deviant as a worthwhile individual, a soul to be saved, but would characterize deviance as immoral, sinful, and self-defeating. It would frown on members who stray, attempt to exert extreme pressure through inner-group loyalty, and display overconformity in the area of deviance itself: this is the pattern frequently encountered in the convert or the reformed sinner. The result is a harsher condemnation of the disapproved behavior than is found in the general population; a fear of the "enlightened," the liberal, and the permissive views, buttressed by a moralistic stance and religion. For those seeking to relinquish their deviance, any suggestion that the consequences of their behavior would be less severe if only social attitudes would change becomes a threat to the organization and its program and a temptation to return to the abandoned pattern. The individuals attracted to such a group are primarily those in need of authority figures and ego reinforcement; these are the compliant and submissive, who nevertheless have a strong component of aggression that will be transferred, during the therapeutic process, from hostility toward society to hostility within the group. As penitents they will both comply and gripe, willingly accept and let off steam.

The second group, those who seek to alleviate the definition of their condition as deviant, consists of people who share only some of the attributes of the former group. And even when sharing them, they do so for entirely different reasons and hence with different consequences. In seeking to change the public attitude toward the deviance, such a group might turn to religion, not for moral support, but for a responsible front and a respectable ally. There would be a reinforcement of the ego, not through group therapy, but through mutual support for deviant values and ways of structuring reality. Middle-class norms would be ridiculed but not entirely rejected, because acceptance by society might be considered easily attainable if one were moralistic, law abiding, and in most respects conforming. The group must thumb its nose at society in order to foster pride in the deviant and at the same time must become obsequious before those in power, in order the better to beg for acceptance. Such a group is likely to attract rebels and nonconformists and yet use a façade of squares and professionals (some of whom may be secret deviants) as front men and window dressing. Its members might vacillate between ultraconformity, as an expression of anticipatory socialization, and rebellion and rejection, as a reaction formation against the society that has cast them out. Because of the enhanced stigmatization that ensues when one joins a group of this type, the organization is likely to attract some neurotics and personality misfits who require social disapproval and ridicule, together with chronic rebels who relish any battle with the world of respectability. Because of the unceasingly aggressive nature of the struggle against society and the small degree of success achieved, such groups are likely to have considerable membership turnover and to suffer bitter internal battles for leadership, fission, competition with other organizations, and the like.

The two types of groups are diametrically opposed in their attitudes toward the deviance with which both are involved. The first group will condemn, moralistically and scientifically, unwaveringly pointing to the eternal damnation that awaits those who slip backward; the second group will likewise invoke science, philosophy, and ideology, but for the eternal condemnation of those who condemn them. The latter type of organization will seek to convince the world without, as well as the members within, that their deviance is normal, natural, moral, socially useful, and that all who deem otherwise are deluded and ignorant hypocrites, self-serving exploiters, or repressed deviants themselves. Both types of group will present a distorted image of themselves; they will fall victim to the temptation, almost inherent in the nature of organization, to project a self-image that glorifies and "prettifies." The first type will show its members as being almost saintly because they are renouncing deviance; by contrast, the devils are not only lost souls who have not seen the light but also opponents in the world of respectability. In the second type of association, there is a glorification of the deviant (member and nonmember alike), and the devils are those in the world of respectability who scoff at such an image.

Of the organizations that exist primarily for the benefit of members, the best known and most successful has been Alcoholics Anonymous. The success of AA and its generally favorable public reception have resulted in the creation of a rash of other groups that attempt to emulate its structure and form, though usually not its content. These include organizations of narcotics addicts, gamblers, self-styled neurotics, and overweight persons. The proliferation of groups of this sort seemed to indicate in some instances that AA had attained a positive status of its own, that it was "proper" to belong, and that belonging meant not only that the stigma of being deviant was being overcome but that a positive esteem was attached if a man or woman had the "ailment" and then was able to renounce it, especially through AA.

The abilities of these organizations to accomplish their manifest goals for individual members have not been examined, except in the cases of AA and Synanon. In the latter instance, one
should note that Synanon has certain structural features that
differentiate it from voluntary associations. It is largely what
Goffman (1961a) has called a "total institution"; in fact, it rejects
addicts who will not relinquish their occupation and life in the
world outside and move in, family and all. The voluntary association is part of one's life, not one's entire life. Synanon should
perhaps better be analyzed as a correctional hospital, offering
group therapy and aid in "kicking the habit," but using unusual
methods to accomplish that goal. It is a hospital in which there
is voluntary self-induction and which depends to an enormous
extent on inner-group norms and loyalties for its success. To
backslide into deviance is to betray the people who have become
one's "family" and who have placed trust in the former addict.

While not all organizational efforts of deviants are directed
toward social change, nevertheless they do have consequences
for the members. The searching out of companions with a similar
problem is suspect; for unlike the alcoholic or the addict, some
of these people did not feel that they had a crippling problem
making them into malfunctioning persons until the organization
caught on and they thought it might be "campy" or "cool" to get
involved. Their organizations, with "anonymity" part of the title,
seem to be the work of poseurs and romantic rebels, who seek
to exploit the status attained by AA rather than to find the
strength to change their own behavior.

The contradiction in this situation would seem to be largely as
follows: whereas AA seeks to build up the self-confidence and
reinforce the egos of members, the act of joining a similar group
of gamblers can accomplish the very reverse. AA infuses in the
individual the belief that alcoholism is an evil he can overcome
to the point of functioning, although he is never free from the
danger of falling back (the warning is an excellent device to retain
the loyalty of the member and thus strengthen the organization).
Hence, for AA there is no category of ex-alcoholics; there are
only "sober alcoholics," the term applying not to people who are
in a temporary and brief state of sobriety between bouts of intoxication but to those who are in a long and, it is hoped, permanent

state of sobriety *after* frequent periods of intoxication. The hold of AA is rooted in the belief that the sober alcoholic is a likely victim for relapse if he is not infused with strength and power, which can best be gained through inner-group cohesion and mutual reinforcement in interaction with others seeking to be saved from the lure of the bottle.

Alcoholics, then, are defined as deviants by others and accept this uncomplimentary view of themselves (a labeling process which, in the ideology of AA, results not in secondary deviance but in rehabilitation). Gamblers—whatever difficulties their habits may cause—are deviants only if they so define themselves, and the act of joining an organization would seem to be a step toward such a definition. Certainly the large number of people who flock to the racetrack, avidly watch for the announcement of the winning number in the daily newspaper, take or give bets in the shop or office, buy government lottery tickets, attend church-sponsored bingo games, frequent betting offices owned and operated by the government, and hopefully follow each day's stock-market gyrations are hardly social deviants. To compare these people with social drinkers, and then to state that the voluntary association is meant to aid compulsive gamblers who are more akin to compulsive alcoholics, offers a point of clarification. However, it is doubtful if the compulsive gambler sees himself as deviant until he joins with others in an organization in which he is compelled to take this view, and the association is therefore as likely to prove ego damaging as ego reinforcing, even if it is successful in aiding some people to overcome their habit (a point which is very doubtful, indeed).

A number of studies have been made of organizations of former mental patients, and for the most part they indicate that such people, meeting great rebuffs and rejection, can find solace in one another. Like alcoholics, they can look to those among the members who have made the most successful adjustments, use these people as role models, and gain encouragement from them. There is a danger that the ex-patient may be more self-blaming when in contact with success that he cannot emulate and that even rehabilitated ex-patients may be so seriously disturbed that they serve as poor models, giving ill-advised counsel that is heeded because it arrives from a big brother—a problem by no means confined to groupings of deviants. By contrast, in an ex-convict group there is a public—and official—suspicion that the mere association of such people with one another is conducive to a return to criminality.

Ex-patient and ex-convict groups have in common the fact that their members have a stigma they are seeking to escape. However, both groups bridge the gap between the two conceptual categories in that both are seeking to live by the norms of society in all respects and at the same time to reduce the hostility society has toward people like themselves. There is no contradiction because they socially define themselves with the prefix "ex-" and view mental patients or convicts not in a derogatory manner but rather with sympathy. They function much as AA does in many respects but have a greater problem convincing the world "out there"—as well as themselves—that they are members of a category that can be trusted to manage their lives. They are unlike AA in that they are not so much involved in changing their own behavior (there is a little of that) as in gaining acceptance. One might say that AA is attempting to turn its members into ex-alcoholics, though it shuns the term, but former mental patients and prisoners who join voluntary organizations are already in the "ex-" category, no matter what further internal change may be seen as desirable.

Of the deviants who have formed voluntary associations in an attempt to influence the society to redefine them as normals, the most prominent are the organized homosexuals. They call their groups "homophile" organizations, a euphemistic term that is meant to project an image of people involved in love relationships with others of the same gender. Organizations of this character indignantly deny the unhealthy, neurotic, or abnormal character of homosexuality, a denial necessary in their view to gain acceptance both from others and among themselves. At the same time, there are many manifestations of the denied neuroticism in the publications and declarations of these organizations: the appeal to sadomasochistic interests is an example. And although the organizations declare that they are not seeking to proselytize for homosexuality, their literature urges that homo-

sexuality be considered on a par with heterosexuality and that
children be exposed to both ways of life in an impartial manner
so as to be able to make a free choice.

Robert Michels, in his classic sociological work *Political Parties*
(1949 ed.), suggests that organizations tend to lose sight of their
original goals and become involved in the struggle for self-per-
petuation, growth of influence, and what today might be called
a greater piece of the action. This would account for the tendency
of almost all organizations of deviants (from AA to the homophile groups) to deny that one is ever really changed or "cured"
—that is, to deny that the ex-alcoholic or the ex-homosexual
exists—and thus to enhance their hold on their followers, who
can never escape from the need for protection. It would also
explain the rivalry that has marked these organizational movements. It would not, however, account for the image put forward,
which is far more acceptable to the public than the effectively
concealed reality. What is occurring here might be conceived of
as a combination of impression management, ideological distor-
tion, and a commonsense approach to public relations; it is found
in political, ethnic, and corporate groups as well as elsewhere,
and it is not confined to deviants, nor is it their special invention.

As protest movements of various types increased in number
and strength in the United States during the 1960s, deviant collectivities increased in militancy. Inspired by the demand for
black power, voices called for gay power; the slogan *Black is
beautiful* received its analogue in *Gay is good.* Despite the obvious
disadvantages of associating with people whose cause has less
than unanimous and enthusiastic appeal, the Black Panthers
made an alliance, however shaky and ephemeral, with homosexuals, and many people in the women's liberation movement
pushed strongly for a similar alliance with lesbians. What seemed
to hold these groups together was their common anti-establish-
ment stance, their unified opposition to oppressive and discriminatory practices.

Organizations of deviants in the end have proved to be one
more strategy for the management of social hostility. If for many
they become a mechanism for escape from deviance, for others
they are an entrapment therein. If they give some people strength
to overcome personally debilitating behavior, to others they give

pride in self and the ego boost of knowing that such behavior has its strong defenders. But this last statement suggests the contradictions in such organizations, and in fact in movements for social change when they do not take on organizational form, for by their propaganda, their ideology, their very existence, they can entrap the neophyte in a world view and outlook that closes the door for him on further growth, development, and change. He may have come out of one closet only to go into another.

7

Social Policy and Norm Violation

NORM VIOLATION AS A PUBLIC ISSUE

It is clear both to the public and to scholars that the violation of some norms goes beyond the limits of public or governmental tolerance. In former times, many such violations were dealt with by the victim and his family and friends: the result was revenge, retribution, and often a cycle of escalating violence. In modern societies, the victim is deprived of the right to assault, rob, or in any other way "get even" with the transgressor, except to a limited extent when he is engaged in self-defense. The victim has relinquished this right, and it has been taken over by the government. Some penal laws involve matters of such importance for the individual and the community that every violation is a public issue. When a girl is raped or a house is burglarized, these are our problems. No one would argue that they have become our problems because busybodies or "moral entrepreneurs" aroused our concern, although it is true that these events are used by some people to arouse fear, hatred, suspicion, and racial tension, in order to achieve their own personal or political ends.

Thus, the act of rape, the single act, is a public issue, but not in the same sense, nor of the same magnitude, as when such acts and others equally intolerable become relatively frequent. That norm violations involving "ordinary crime," "street crime," crimes against individuals and their property have reached the proportion of a major social problem in the United States is hardly deniable.

Some argue, with considerable force and effect, that political crimes committed by those in power, crimes by corporations and by powerful and wealthy individuals, white-collar and upper-world crimes go relatively unnoticed and if apprehended are only mildly punished. Such acts are no doubt as harmful to society as are acts of burglary and robbery but are treated with less concern, not only because they are committed by those in the palaces of power but also because they do not affect you and me, as individuals, so directly and in so frightening a manner. We may lose more money over a period of time because of the bribery of political persons, because of the corruption of corporate executives, because of price fixing and fee splitting, than we might if a wallet were taken by a mugger. But the larcenous acts of the rich and mighty are not accompanied by fear and fright and take place subtly, often without our knowledge of their existence. No wonder, then, that it is the ordinary crime that has become a public issue, resulting in a great outcry, ranging from those who call for widespread social change in order to make the society less criminogenic to those who see no immediate solution other than locking up the violators and, for all practical purposes, throwing away the keys.

Sometimes society is seen as overreacting to victimless deviance. The advocates of decriminalization argue that many types of deviant acts have no victims; that is, that no one is hurt except possibly those who voluntarily commit the acts, that the acts can be tolerated without great damage to the society, and that legalization will aid in combatting the police corruption and organized criminal activities that often accompany illegal acts for which there is great demand and so many customers. Finally, there is no general consensus in society (as there is for rape and burglary) that these types of activities must be illegal or even that they are improper, wrong, or sinful. In short, it is believed that they are not the law's business and, even if they are not socially desirable, should not be held illegal, and the persons involved in them should not be held accountable to the police, the courts, and the legal system.

This position has been taken by many people with regard to consensual sexual behavior between or among adults, the use of marijuana and even heroin, the distribution of hard-core pornography, and other activities that have traditionally been held to be the business of the law. Opponents of decriminalization have not only opposed these activities and claimed that they are socially harmful but also have argued that the purpose of the law is to make official a view that certain types of conduct are immoral. Law, in other words, is the codification of morality. The adherents of decriminalization, in addition to showing the benefits to the society of ceasing to make these and other acts illegal, state that there is an alternative between the urge to condemn and the urge to condone. This alternative would be, apparently, the road of education, of discouragement of activities found or believed to be harmful, such as suicide, for example, or alcoholism.

Decriminalization as a Process

Application of the concept of decriminalization involves more than the effort to repeal a law and remove its penal sanctions. The law must have carried with it the notion of criminality, for without it there can be no decriminalization. Once that problem is disposed of, decriminalization goes through several stages, but it meets impediments and arouses conflicts and countermovements.

Sometimes it is achieved by simple obsolescence. A law remains on the books, but legal and judicial authorities may have forgotten its existence or may have decided deliberately to disregard it. Under such circumstances, the law's capacity for causing mischief is relatively slight, although the very fact that it is retained gives it some potential for inflicting harm on the transgressor. The Sunday blue laws came to be disregarded, and important civil-rights legislation enacted following the Civil War was allowed to fall into disuse, forgotten by all but a few faithful militants and revived under the pressure of the civil-rights movement when it was "needed."

There is a danger of innocent victimization and harassment when unused laws are allowed to remain on the books and an act becomes decriminalized merely through obsolescence, indifference, and disuse. This situation facilitates the victimization of someone, not because he has violated the particular law (this he may have done, but usually no one cares), but because he espouses unpopular ideas, or because of race or creed. This is illustrated in the case of Father Philip Berrigan and Sister Elizabeth McAllister, two antiwar activists. Together with several of their colleagues, they were indicted and tried on a number of charges, including conspiracy to commit sabotage and to kidnap a prominent person in the Nixon Administration. Although the jury was unable to agree on the major charges (which were subsequently dropped), the two defendants were convicted and sentenced for unauthorized correspondence from a federal prison, in violation of a law that had not been enforced for many years.

A second and clearly related method of transforming the status of an act from criminal to noncriminal can occur without legislative action and without legal repeal, through new judicial interpretations of the law, often to conform with changing public opinion. In some instances legislation long on the books may be declared unconstitutional, although this can be considered a mechanism for repeal. More frequently, with changing public attitudes and new concepts of morality, novel interpretations of the law are given by courts that are sensitive to political and social upheavals, a process made possible by the loose manner in which the laws were originally written. Most of the laws against public indecent exposure and pornography were not repealed; what changed were the standards and criteria by which certain objects, people, or behavior fell within these forbidden purviews. Progressively liberal or permissive decisions were for a time handed down by the United States Supreme Court and other federal and state courts.

These are instances of decriminalization by means of a law's falling into disuse or by a series of decisions, usually gradual, and often following changes in public opinion. Developments of this type are interactive and circularly dynamic, with the modified attitudes resulting in new legal decisions and the latter resulting in further modification of the attitudes. The spiral can travel in the other direction, however, as when the decisions of the courts bring about behavior for which the public is unprepared and a backlash ensues.

If there is strong conflict of opinion, not so much about the law but about the propriety of the act itself, this may give rise to a social movement for decriminalization. Such a force can take hold essentially under two conditions: (1) when there is a diminishing sense of moral rigidity concerning the activity and (2) when people have become convinced that the law either has not succeeded in diminishing the act or has brought with it substantial secondary evils. In other words, the criminal sanctions should be removed in some instances, it is argued, because the mores have changed (or perhaps the moral outlook never was what the legislators made it out to be) or because, although the mores have not changed, there is recognition that society suffers more from the effects of illegality than from the action that has been outlawed.

Several examples will illustrate these general statements. Abortion reform became viable as a result of changed attitudes; homosexual law reform, as a result of a wide feeling that "it's his business, not mine." Laws against miscegenation were repealed both because of a political movement that made all racially discriminatory legislation difficult to defend and embarrassing to American society and because it was felt that this was a proper matter for social but not legal action. Most but not all arguments for the legalization of hard drugs stress that greater evil flows from the illegalization than from the drugs themselves, whereas movements for the repeal of marijuana restrictions stress the harmlessness of smoking marijuana.

The struggle for law reform is often a mechanism for conducting another and more important struggle, that is, for a change in public attitude, for destigmatization. While there is a great deal of discrimination, both official and unofficial, against people suspected of practicing homosexuality, the harassment is less legal than social. There are relatively few arrests in the United States for consensual adult homosexual activity in private; the arrests are for such acts in semipublic places, for public solicitation, and, until the early 1970s, for the congregation of "undesirables" in various public places, such as gay bars.

The laws themselves give rise to social movements for their repeal. In a sense, these movements consist of moral entrepreneurs of the liberal persuasion, analogous to the crusaders described by Becker (1963), who take it upon themselves to campaign for repressive legislation. The movement distributes its propaganda, issues press releases, gets exposure on the mass media, campaigns, lobbies, enters political battles, all to arouse public ire over the injustices and the potential for harm if the law is continued. The struggle proceeds, in fact, along a two-pronged line of attack, emphasizing not only the harm brought about by the law but also the good that could be accomplished by the illegal act if only it were allowed to flower in full light of day.

The Nature of Secondary Crime

An unenforced law does not have to give rise to secondary crime, but, as Schur (1965) points out, when there is a strong demand for the service (such as abortion, prostitution, or gambling) and it continues to thrive in a subterranean network, new and greater crimes will be committed. However, it is an error to see decriminalization as a panacea; some of this secondary crime would thrive even if the act were legal.

For example, blackmail is often associated with homosexuality. It may be true that some blackmail would not be possible if there were no anti-homosexual laws, but the blackmail comes primarily from stigmatization, secrecy, and the threat of exposure, with the potential damage to social, familial, and financial relationships, and these could be present without laws. In England for long periods of time there were no laws against homosexuality, but blackmail appears nevertheless to have thrived during those times. Adultery may give rise to a good deal of blackmail because a man's marriage or career would be threatened by exposure; the question of criminality is irrelevant.

The outstanding secondary crime resulting from the search for an illegal commodity is found in the area of narcotics. Illegalization drives the price of hard drugs incredibly high, and since most users are unable to support their habit by gainful employment, they resort to mugging and thievery (often victimizing their own families, at least at the start), prostitution, and drug pushing to obtain funds. It is said that in the early 1970s New York City had 150,000 to 200,000 drug users. If the average habit cost twenty dollars a day to support, they would require a total of three to four million dollars' worth daily. Regular employment, prostitution and other "victimless crimes," and marginal methods of making money other than burglary and thievery might account for—at most—one-fifth of this. That would leave about two million dollars a day to be obtained by addicts in an illegal manner. In England, by contrast, although there is some illegal trafficking in drugs, legal dispensing to registered addicts has almost entirely eliminated the problem of thievery for the purpose of supporting a drug habit.

There is a great deal of violence associated with the worlds of prostitution and homosexuality, in part, perhaps, the result of fly-by-night relationships, anonymity, and to some extent the psychological problems gripping people involved in this type of sexual encounter. However, it would require destigmatization to reduce substantially this peripheral and tangential crime, although decriminalization would be a step toward such diminution.

A Crisis of Overcriminalization

Sanford Kadish (1967) refers to the American situation as "a crisis of overcriminalization," and indeed this is no exaggeration. What makes it a crisis is not only the tremendous number of restrictive laws (something not rare in other countries) but also the widespread disregard for these laws, their flagrant violation, and their lack of support by considerable portions of the population.

The United States is suffering from high crime rates, insufficient police forces, lack of confidence in the integrity of the police by large portions of the populace, extremely long pretrial detention for those unable to put up bail, the admitted evils of plea bargaining, crowded court calendars, and the phenomenon of very crowded jails and prisons while large numbers of criminals walk the streets or hold government office.

Many of these evils could be eliminated by decriminalization, but not all. Drunkenness accounts for approximately half the arrests in America in any single year. An urban society cannot ignore the public (and particularly the chronic) inebriate. To stop seeing such persons in the criminal context and to stop sending them through a court system (with its revolving-door policy and its two-minute trials that make a mockery of criminal justice) would necessitate the substitution of social workers, paramedical personnel, and clinics for the present system. While this would diminish congestion in courtrooms and jails, other facilities would be required to take their place. The *Uniform Crime Reports* would no longer show so many arrests, but this would constitute a spurious reduction in crime. It is not even certain that the police could be relieved of handling such persons, for if intoxication were no longer a legal matter, it would unburden the police only if no tasks had to be performed to take care of alcoholics or if other persons were available for that purpose.

Decriminalization has many attractive features, but it does not solve the basic behavioral problem that is involved unless that problem is one that requires no other solution than legalization. The most important aspect of decriminalization, other than re-lieving the society of the burden of secondary criminality, may be that it will *assist* in lifting the stigma of crime from many who are now outcasts. But even this partial effect cannot be accomplished automatically by repeal of law, as if by a magic wand. It will require education to help people who have been outcasts to come back and be welcomed into society. Except for those activities that are defined by people as positive and to be encouraged, or neutral and not be discouraged, the problem will persist in a new and sometimes even more acute form: the channeling of behavior into socially acceptable and useful ways when people behaving in another fashion are treated neither as criminals nor as social outcasts.

DEVIANCE, DIVERSITY, AND SOCIAL CHANGE

In the film "Lenny," based on the life of a man who combined comedy with social criticism, Lenny Bruce is shown being dragged out of court after pleading with a judge to listen to his explanation of why he was using obscene language in a public performance at a time when doing so was strictly tabooed. The judge orders Bruce to be silent and then asks that he be physically removed from the court. While being dragged off by the marshals, Lenny yells out, "I'm a deviant, I'm a deviant, the society needs deviants."

If these words were actually shouted in court, and very likely they were, Lenny Bruce, more social protester than sociologist, might have meant merely that he did things in a manner that was different from the ways of others, and that diversity was good for society. But if he had had sociological training and was using the word *deviant* as professionals use it, he could have been even more accurate. For, at the time, he was transgressing, violating the most elementary rules of propriety in the United States. In public, with a microphone in hand, and before an audience of men and women, there was not a forbidden word that he did not utter, and not a subject that was off limits to him. For this act, he drew down upon himself the wrath of a portion of the society, those who had handcuffs, keys to the jails, and seats several feet higher than all others in their rooms: in short, the people in power. Flouting their rules and flaunting his violations, he was indeed a deviant, and one who was useful to a society that at the time was still bound by fears of words, enshrouding some vital subjects in secrecy for the public while they were widely discussed in private. The deviance of Lenny Bruce was a challenge to the old ways of society, a dramatic manner of compelling the powers that made the rules to reexamine their rules and their ways. A few years after his early death, Bruce's manner of speech was widely used in the arts, on stage and screen, where a few decades before one could not say *damn* without fear of giving offense; and it is largely to the exploratory efforts of Bruce and others like him that this social change can be attributed.

The norms are there, and sometimes they are written into law. But societies either undergo change, or change is retarded by slow-moving and fearful politicians, by religious or educational institutions, by people with a vested interest in maintaining the status quo. Deviance, in two senses, constitutes a challenge to the old ways, a clarion call for reevaluating what was once taken for granted as correct. The first is illustrated by the case of Lenny Bruce: the deviant confronts society, compels people to reflect on what they have been doing, and forces an open conflict between different ways. In the area of race relations and civil rights, the deviants were those (of various racial and ethnic identities) who refused to accept discrimination, inequality, and the flouting of the Constitution. Martin Luther King, Jr., was such a deviant, and his strategy was to compel a confrontation between his ways and the norms of the white power structure. Homosexuals, among others, have tried to change what they consider outmoded norms, by seeking public acceptance of the deviant way.

But deviance can serve to correct the evils of a society in another manner. A large amount of unacceptable deviance, of a type that falls outside the limits of what a society can tolerate (murder or rape, for example), while it cannot and should not result in relaxing the norms and accepting the formerly disapproved behavior, can arouse people to see that something is basically wrong with the entire structure of society. Whether it be the economic, political, educational, familial, or some other aspect of the society, whether it be because of racial inequality or because of the failure to replace religion with a secular morality, the wrongs are seen in sharp relief because of the frequency with which important norms are flouted.

This is not to suggest that basic social change can best come about through planned deviance. While lawbreaking may lead to a study of the social roots of certain events, it can also result in repressive measures from which everyone—the criminal, the victim, and the populace at large—suffers. Furthermore, unlike the use of obscene language by Lenny Bruce or the acts of people living together openly without benefit of state or clergy, some norm violations bring about victimization so intolerable that a better way ought to have been found to change aspects of the social structure. If the Watergate scandal were to result in a genuine resurgence of morality in the political arena, it would have been a small price to pay to correct the corruption of people in power. But if the thirty years of Vietnam results in an end to American (and other) military intervention abroad, who can say that the hundreds of thousands of Indochinese and American fatalities were worth this result? If the war dead could rise up and speak, would they not say that another, less costly road could have been found to promote nonintervention and peace?

Emile Durkheim saw crime and deviance as being useful to societies, in that such disapproved behavior helped identify the limits of acceptable behavior by dramatically distinguishing it from the unacceptable. Not only was deviance boundary-maintaining but, in excluding the deviant from the life of a community or society, by killing or banishing or in later years imprisoning him, the punishments act to arouse a sense of indignation and to unite the "good people." If it is applicable to modern societies at all (Durkheim based much of his approach on the studies of homogeneous primitive societies), it accounts not for norm violation but for the deliberate effort of a power group to arouse a public against an imagined or fantasied outgroup. Thus Erikson (1966) was able to apply the Durkheim approach to the Salem witchcraft trials. But in this instance the society was literally creating the deviance. In more recent times, anti-Semitism undoubtedly played a large part in uniting the German people under the Hitler regime, but such social cohesion can hardly be evaluated as a social good. Durkheim lived before the age of totalitarianism, although not of tyrants, and his glorification of cohesion would hardly be echoed by social thinkers in the last quarter of the twentieth century.

So that one can summarize by saying that deviance can have functional consequences, but not necessarily so. Laws and norms should always be viewed with skepticism, by each new group that comes into a society, by each new generation that looks at the ways into which it has been socialized.

One should be wary, however, of confusing iconoclasts, those who shake their fists at the old ways, who live by their own standards without harm to others (or to themselves, for that matter), with people whose acts cannot be tolerated. Not all deviance is diversity. A society needs and thrives on diversity; it develops and grows with the conflict between different ideas, views, and ways of life. Its social institutions are better if they have articulate critics who denounce the way things are and set an example of or at least advocate different ways.

Then, perhaps, one can reconcile on a society-wide basis the conflict mentioned earlier, on a personal basis: the conflict between hostility to the conformist and hostility to the deviant. It is unfortunate that the word *conformist* has come to be associated with slavish Babbittry, with overrigidity, fear of individualism, terror at the prospect that anyone will disapprove, inability to think for oneself. But one can conform to most of the ways of society because one believes them to be right, necessary, or unimportant and not worth the hassle of violating them; and one can go off in other directions when this will add to the diversity of both the individual and of society. This, we believe, is the lesson to be learned from the study of norms and their relationship to human behavior.

References

Akers, Ronald L. "Problems in the sociology of deviance: social definitions and behavior." *Social Forces* 46 (1968):455–65.

Barnard, Chester. *The Functions of the Executive.* Cambridge, Mass.: Harvard University Press, 1938.

Becker, Howard S. *Outsiders: Studies in the Sociology of Deviance.* New York: Free Press, 1963.

Becker, Howard S., et al. *Boys in White.* Chicago: University of Chicago Press, 1961.

Beigel, Hugo G. "A weekend in Alice's wonderland." *Journal of Sex Research* 5 (1969):108–22.

Bonger, William A. *An Introduction to Criminology.* London: Methuen, 1932.

Broyard, Anatole. "Portrait of the inauthentic Negro: how prejudice distorts the victim's personality." *Commentary* 10 (1950):56–64.

Cameron, Mary Owen. *The Booster and the Snitch.* New York: Free Press, 1964.

Cohen, Alfred K. *Deviance and Control.* Englewood Cliffs, N.J.: Prentice-Hall, 1966.

Davis, Fred. "Deviance disavowal: the management of strained interaction by the visibly handicapped." *Social Problems* 9 (1961):120–32.

Davis, Kingsley. "The sociology of parent-youth conflict." *American Sociological Review* 5 (1940):523–35.

Durkheim, Emile. *The Division of Labor in Society.* New York: Macmillan, 1933.

Erikson, Kai T. "A comment on disguised observation in sociology." *Social Problems* 14 (Spring 1967):366–73.

――――. *Wayward Puritans: A Study in the Sociology of Deviance.* New York: Wiley, 1966.

Ferracuti, Franco. "European migration and crime." In Marvin E. Wolfgang, ed., *Crime and Culture: Essays in Honor of Thorsten Sellin.* New York: Wiley, 1968.

Gans, Herbert J. *The Urban Villagers: Group and Class in the Life of Italo-Americans.* New York: Free Press, 1962.

Garfinkel, Harold. "Conditions of successful degradation ceremonies." *American Journal of Sociology* 61 (1956):420–24.

――――. *Studies in Ethnomethodology.* Englewood Cliffs, N.J.: Prentice-Hall, 1967.

Gibbs, Jack P. "Norms: the problem of definition and classification." *American Journal of Sociology* 70 (1965):586–94.

Glueck, Sheldon. "Theory and fact in criminology." *British Journal of Delinquency* 7 (October 1956):92–98.

Goffman, Erving. *The Presentation of Self in Everyday Life.* Garden City, N.Y.: Doubleday, 1959.

――――. *Asylums: Essays on the Social Situations of Mental Patients and Other Inmates.* Garden City, N.Y.: Doubleday, 1961a.

――――. *Encounters.* Indianapolis, Ind.: Bobbs-Merrill, 1961b.

――――. *Stigma: Notes on the Management of Spoiled Identity.* Englewood Cliffs, N.J.: Prentice-Hall, 1963.

――――. *Interaction Ritual.* Garden City, N.Y.: Doubleday Anchor, 1967.

――――. *Strategic Interaction.* Philadelphia: University of Pennsylvania Press, 1969.

――――. *Relations in Public,* New York: Basic Books, 1972.

Goode, Erich. *The Marijuana Smokers.* New York: Basic Books, 1970.

Gouldner, Alvin. *Patterns of Industrial Bureaucracy.* Glencoe, Ill.: Free Press, 1954.

Hartjen, Clayton A. *Crime and Criminalization.* New York: Praeger, 1974.

Hobsbawm, E. J. *Primitive Rebels: Studies in Archaic Forms of Social Movement in the 19th and 20th Centuries.* New York: Praeger, 1963.

Hoffman, Martin. *The Gay World: Male Homosexuality and the Social Creation of Evil.* New York: Basic Books, 1968.

Kadish, Sanford. "The crisis of overcriminalization." *The Annals of the American Academy of Political and Social Science* 374 (1967):157–70.

Kitsuse, John I. "Societal reaction to deviant behavior: problems of theory and method." *Social Problems* 9 (1962):247–56.

Kittrie, Nicholas N. *The Right to Be Different: Deviance and Enforced Therapy.* Baltimore: Johns Hopkins Press, 1971.

Lemert, Edwin M. *Social Pathology: A Systematic Approach to the Theory of Sociopathic Behavior.* New York: McGraw-Hill, 1951.

_____. "Social structure, social control, and deviation." In Marshall B. Clinard, ed., *Anomie and Deviant Behavior: A Discussion and Critique,* New York: Free Press, 1964.

Lofland, John. *Deviance and Identity.* Englewood Cliffs, N.J.: Prentice-Hall, 1967.

Lorber, Judith. "Deviance as performance: the case of illness." *Social Problems* 14 (1967):302–10.

Mankoff, Milton. "Societal reaction and career deviance: a critical analysis." *Sociological Quarterly* 12 (1971):204–18.

Marcuse, Herbert. "Comments on Watergate." *New York Times,* June 27, 1973, p. 39.

Marx, Karl. *Theories of Surplus Value.* Part I. Moscow: Progress Publishers, 1963.

Matza, David. *Delinquency and Drift.* New York: Wiley, 1964.

Mead, George Herbert. *Mind, Self and Society.* Chicago: University of Chicago Press, 1934.

Mead, Margaret. *And Keep Your Powder Dry.* New York: Morrow, 1965.

Merton, Robert K. "The self-fulfilling prophecy." *Antioch Review* 8 (Summer 1948):193–210.

_____. "Social structure and anomie." *American Sociological Review* 3 (1938):672–82.

_____. *Social Theory and Social Structure.* rev. ed., New York: Free Press, 1957.

Michels, Robert. *Political Parties: A Sociological Study of the Oligarchical Tendencies of Modern Democracy.* Glencoe, Ill.: Free Press, 1949.

Niederhoffer, Arthur. *Behind the Shield: The Police in Urban Society.* Garden City, N.Y.: Doubleday, 1967.

Quinney, Richard. *The Social Reality of Crime.* Boston: Little, Brown, 1970.

Roszak, Theodore. *The Making of a Counter Culture: Reflections on the Technocratic Society and Its Youthful Opposition.* Garden City, N.Y.: Doubleday, 1969.

Rudé, George F. E. *The Crowd in the French Revolution.* Oxford: Clarendon Press, 1969.

Sagarin, Edward. *Deviants and Deviance: An Introduction to the Study of Disvalued People and Behavior.* New York: Praeger, 1975.

Scheff, Thomas J. *Being Mentally Ill: A Sociological Theory.* Chicago: Aldine, 1966.

Scheler, Max. *Ressentiment*. New York: Free Press, 1961.

Schur, Edwin M. *Crimes without Victims: Deviant Behavior and Public Policy —Abortion, Homosexuality and Drug Addiction*. Englewood Cliffs, N.J.: Prentice-Hall, 1965.

————. *Labeling Deviant Behavior: Its Sociological Implications*. New York: Harper & Row, 1971.

Schutz, Alfred. *Collected Papers*. The Hague: Martinus Nijhoff, 1964.

Sellin, Thorsten. *Culture Conflict and Crime*. New York: Social Science Research Council, 1938.

————, and Marvin E. Wolfgang. *The Measurement of Delinquency*. New York: Wiley, 1964.

Shoham, Shlomo. *Crime and Social Deviation*. Chicago: Henry Regnery, 1966.

Sumner, William Graham. *Folkways: A Study of the Sociological Importance of Usages, Manners, Customs, Mores, and Morals*. Boston: Ginn, 1906.

Sutherland, Edwin H. "White-collar criminality." *American Sociological Review* 5 (1940):1–12.

————. *Criminology*. 3rd ed., Philadelphia: Lippincott, 1939.

Szasz, Thomas S. *The Manufacture of Madness: A Comparative Study of the Inquisition and the Mental Health Movement*. New York: Harper & Row, 1970.

Tannenbaum, Frank. *Crime and the Community*. Boston: Ginn, 1938.

Tappan, Paul W. "Who is the criminal?" *American Sociological Review* 12 (1947):96–102.

Tarde, Gabriel. *Penal Philosophy*. 1912. Reprinted, Montclair, N.J.: Patterson Smith, 1968.

Thompson, E. P. *The Making of the English Working Class*. New York: Pantheon, 1964.

Thorsell, Bernard A., and Lloyd W. Klemke. "The labeling process: reinforcement and deterrent?" *Law and Society Review* 6 (1972)-:393–403.

Toffler, Alvin. *Future Shock*. New York: Random House, 1970.

Torrey, E. Fuller. *The Mind Game: Witchdoctors and Psychiatrists*. New York: Bantam, 1973.

Turner, Ralph H. "Deviance avowal as neutralization of commitment." *Social Problems* 19 (1972):308–21.

Weber, Max. *The Protestant Ethic and the Spirit of Capitalism*. New York: Scribner's, 1959.

Williams, Robin M. *American Society: A Sociological Interpretation*. New York: Alfred A. Knopf, 1960.

Winick, Charles. "Physician narcotic addicts." *Social Problems* 9 (1961): 174–86.

Wirth, Louis. *On Cities and Social Life: Selected Papers.* Chicago: University of Chicago Press, 1964.

Yinger, J. Milton. "Contraculture and subculture." *American Sociological Review* 25 (1960):625–35.

Index